**Quality Excellence for Suppliers of
Telecommunications
Leadership Forum**

# TL 9000 Quality System
# Requirements

# Book One
## Release 2.5

# Foreword

The Telecommunications industry service providers and their suppliers are committed to meeting the expectations of their customers. Each has strived individually to accomplish this for many years. Most observers of the telecommunications industry would agree that very good progress has been made in the twentieth century. There is also a strong need, however, for even greater progress in the years ahead, and the challenge is how to make this a reality.

The Quality Excellence for Suppliers of Telecommunications Forum includes most of the major service providers and their suppliers. We have joined forces in a remarkably cooperative and constructive spirit and created the TL 9000 Handbooks. Our goal from the beginning has been to develop a consistent set of quality system requirements and metrics when implemented will help provide telecommunications users with faster, better and more cost-effective services.

The TL 9000 Quality System Requirements and TL 9000 Quality System Metrics Handbooks were produced by having the best people from service providers and suppliers working together toward a common goal. The handbooks include an agreed-upon set of quality system requirements and metrics that were drawn from the best features of similar management system standards and the most effective quality practices currently being used in the telecommunications industry.

As we in the telecommunications industry take steps to ensure that the quality of our services keeps pace with changing technological opportunities in the twenty-first century, all telecommunications users worldwide will benefit from ever improving telecommunications products.


**Steve Welch**
QuEST Forum – Chairman

**Krish Prabhu**
QuEST Forum – Vice Chair

# Preface

The Quality Excellence for Suppliers of Telecommunications Leadership Forum ("QuEST Forum") was founded to foster continued improvements to the quality and reliability of telecommunications service. The founders took the critical initial step of establishing a common set of quality system requirements and metrics by creating the *TL 9000 Quality System Requirements Handbook* and the *TL 9000 Quality System Metrics Handbook*. These handbooks are the result of a cooperative effort among members of the telecommunications industry.

The work of the QuEST Forum yields benefits to service providers, their subscribers, and their suppliers. Membership is composed of members of the telecommunications industry. Members fund and participate in the Forum, have defined voting rights and are expected to contribute to the work of the Forum. Members vote on adoption of the TL 9000 structure, content, administration and other questions coming before the Forum.

The Forum establishes and maintains a common set of quality system requirements and metrics built upon currently used industry standards, including the ISO 9001 International Standard. The requirements promote consistency, efficiency, and improve customer satisfaction. They also enable suppliers to improve quality and reliability, reduce costs and increase competitiveness.

# Acknowledgements

Many members of the Quality Excellence for Suppliers of Telecommunications Forum ("QuEST Forum") contributed to the development of the *TL 9000 Handbooks*. These handbooks were truly a team effort by the experts that make up the Forum's membership. The following individuals participated in the development of this set of TL 9000 Quality System Requirements as representatives of their companies.

I would like to thank the members of the QuEST Forum and the volunteer registrars for their dedication and cooperation in creating the TL 9000 Handbooks, and the Quality Excellence for Suppliers of Telecommunications Forum.

*J McDonnell*

Jim McDonnell
QuEST Forum Project Director

| | | | |
|---|---|---|---|
| Daniel Avery | Symmetricom | Duke Dahmen | Tellabs |
| Galen Aycock | Bell Atlantic | Ashok Dandekar | Fujitsu |
| Beth Baker | AIAG | Paula DeCarlo | Pulsecom |
| Chanden Banerjee | Newbridge Networks | E. deVries | Telkom South Africa |
| Bret Barclay | RELTEC Corp. | Thierno Diallo | 3M Telecom Systems |
| Jim Barke | ADC Telecommunications | Bob Dietz | RELTEC Corp. |
| Alan Beaudry | Bell Atlantic | Tim Dinneen | Sprint North Supply |
| Gary Bishop | Sumitomo Electric | Amy Dixon | Lucent Technologies |
| Dave Bisone | Lucent Technologies | Allen Dobney | Cisco Systems |
| Reg Blake | BSI | Kim Dobson | Motorola |
| Terry Blok | Unisys | Joe Doro | Charles Industries |
| James Bossert | Nokia Mobile Phones | Jean-Normand Drouin | Bell Canada |
| Michele Boulanger | Motorola | Jim Dumouchelle | Nortel Networks |
| Paula Brackman | Telcordia Technologies | Greg Feldman | Motorola |
| Bob Brigham | Telcordia Technologies | Mehmet Ficici | QUASAR |
| Joan Brough-Kerrebyn | SCC | Paul Fortlage | RAB |
| Jack Burgen | MCI WorldCom | Tilman Foust | Hekimian Laboratories |
| Larry Busch | Lucent Technologies | Ed Franck | Ameritech |
| Jerry Cates | Siecor | Barbara Frank | Alcatel |
| Bob Cicelski | Newbridge Networks | Ken Gale | Nortel Networks |
| Francois Coallier | Bell Canada | Mike Gericke | BellSouth |
| Bud Cuthbert | QMI | Joe Gibbs | Lucent Technologies |

| | | | |
|---|---|---|---|
| Frank Gray, Jr. | Motorola | Bill Poliseo | BVQI |
| Robert Gray | AT&T | Tex Prater | BellSouth |
| Glen Groenewold | Motorola | Richard Pratt | Ericsson |
| Dennis Grousosky | Graybar Electric | Jodie Pryor | AT&T |
| Jack Growe | CTDI | Judy Przekop | Ameritech |
| Steve Hackett | SBC | Misha Ptak | Pulsecom |
| Jeff Harpe | Nortel Networks | Mustafa Pulat | Lucent Technologies |
| Andy Hart | BroadBand Technologies | George Raemore | Motorola |
| Debbie Hearn | Telcordia Technologies | Soundar Rajan | PairGain Technologies |
| Rich Helmuth | GTE | Gary Reams | NEC America |
| Ron Hershberger | Ericsson | Joel Reece | Siecor |
| Gene Hutchison | SBC | Bridget Rees | NEC America |
| Steve Jackson | Westell | Jerry Reichert | RELTEC Corp. |
| Ari Jain | Lucent Technologies | Donna Reinsch | RELTEC Corp. |
| Alka Jarvis | Cisco Systems | John Rosenow | MCI WorldCom |
| John Jennings | RELTEC Corp | Gwynne Roshon-Larsen | Cisco Systems |
| Mike Jennings | Pulsecom | Marty Rudnick | Lucent Technologies |
| Pete Johnson | Graybar Electric | John Russell | Telcordia Technologies |
| John J. Johnson IV | Pulsecom | H. Pierre Salle | KEMA |
| Wally Jubran | Pirelli | Mike Samocki | Teltrend |
| Tim Kalisz | Telcordia Technologies | Victor Sandoval | Ericsson |
| Mary-Ruth Keough | Alcatel | Donna Schilling | Symmetricom |
| Duane Knecht | CTDI | Tom Scurlock | Lucent Technologies |
| Ken Koffman | Siemens | Darryl Seeley | RELTEC Corp. |
| Jeff Lanham | Sprint | Chris Shillito | Eagle Registrations |
| Gene Lassiter | Nortel Networks | David Siebrasse | Antec |
| Sandy Liebesman | Lucent Technologies | Doug Smith | Ericsson |
| Matt Lindsay | Tellabs | John Smith | Tellabs |
| Ron Luttrull | Alcatel | John Snarr | RELTEC Corp. |
| Richard Lycette | Newbridge Networks | Phil Snow | Alcatel |
| Nick Magro | Underwriters Laboratories | Roy Stephens | PairGain Technologies |
| Dick Malcangio | Qualcomm | Rob Stewart | Cisco Systems |
| Henry Malec | 3COM | Olga Striltschuk | Motorola |
| Michael Manning | Newbridge Networks | Steve Stroup | SBC |
| Sue Maxwell | Excel Switching | Joel Sullivan | BellSouth |
| Tama McBride | Motorola | Greg Swan | BVQI |
| Jim McDonnell | SBC | Bill Taylor | Antec |
| Greg Miller | Motorola | Joe Taylor | Tellabs |
| Paul Miller | Siemens | Steve Thoma | GTE |
| Ken Molenilli | RELTEC Corp. | Don Topper | Alcatel |
| Mark Moore | Alcatel | Anthony Vitucci | Hekimian |
| Art Morrical | Lucent Technologies | Vicki Walker | Tellabs |
| Rosemarie Moskow | SBC | John Walz | Lucent Technologies |
| Pat Muirragui | Siemens | Tom Wanek | RELTEC Corp. |
| Tom Murrell | Pirelli | Rich Watts | AT&T |
| John Nolan | US West | Rick Werth | SBC |
| William J. Novak | Lucent Technologies | Randal Whorton | ADTRAN |
| Charles O'Donnell | ADTRAN | Don Wilford | US WEST |
| Robert Oakley | Nortel Networks | John Wronka | Lucent Technologies |
| Kathy Parker | AT&T | Leslie Wolf | Telcordia Technologies |
| Robert Paschke | MCI WorldCom | Tom Yohe | Alcatel |
| Brendan Pelan | Bell Atlantic | Len Young | Corning |
| Nat Perkinson | BroadBand Technologies | Mark Young | Siemens |
| Richard Pierrie | Nortel Networks | | |

# Table of Contents

# List of Figures

# List of Tables

# Section 1 – Introduction

The TL 9000 Handbooks (TL 9000 Quality System Requirements and the TL 9000 Quality System Metrics) are designed specifically for the telecommunications industry to document the industry's quality system requirements and metrics.

The TL 9000 Quality System Requirements Handbook consists of four (4) major sections with appendices. It establishes a common set of quality system requirements for suppliers of telecommunications products: hardware, software or services. The requirements are built upon existing industry standards, including ISO 9001. The TL 9000 Quality System Metrics Handbook defines a minimum set of performance metrics and cost and quality indicators to measure progress and evaluate results of quality system implementation.

## 1.1 Goals

The goals of TL 9000 are to:
- Foster quality systems that effectively and efficiently protect the integrity and use of telecommunications products: hardware, software or services;
- Establish and maintain a common set of quality system requirements;
- Reduce the number of telecommunications quality system standards;
- Define effective cost and performance-based metrics to guide progress and evaluate results of quality system implementation;
- Drive continuous improvement;
- Enhance customer-supplier relationships; and
- Leverage industry conformity assessment processes.

## 1.2 Purpose

The purpose of TL 9000 is to define the telecommunications quality system requirements for the design, development, production, delivery, installation, and maintenance of products: hardware, software or services. Included in TL 9000 are cost and performance-based metrics that measure reliability and quality performance of these products.

## 1.3 Benefits of Implementation

Telecommunications service providers, their subscribers, and all customers will benefit as a result of implementing TL 9000.

Expected benefits are:
- Continuous improvement of service to subscribers;
- Enhanced customer-supplier relationships;
- Standardization of quality system requirements;
- Efficient management of external audits and site visits;
- Uniform cost and performance-based metrics;
- Overall cost reduction and increased competitiveness;
- Enhanced management and improvement of supplier's performance; and
- Industry benchmarks for TL 9000 metrics.

## 1.4 Relationship to ISO 9001 and Other Requirements

The QuEST Forum maintains compatibility with other sets of requirements and standards. TL 9000 provides a telecommunications-specific set of requirements built upon an ISO 9001:1994 framework. See the Bibliography for the standards and requirements that were considered during the development of TL 9000.

Characteristics of the TL 9000 relationship to other requirements are:

- TL 9000 includes ISO 9001:1994; any future revisions to ISO 9001 will be incorporated;
- Conformance to TL 9000 constitutes conformance to corresponding ISO 9001 requirements; and
- It is the intent of the QuEST Forum that conformance to TL 9000 will eliminate the need for conformance to other telecommunications quality management standards.

## 1.5 Customer-Supplier Communication

TL 9000 requires a supplier to establish and maintain a process for communicating with its customer base; refer to Section 4, requirement 4.21.2. Also see the Appendix, "Guidance for Customer-Supplier Communications."

## 1.6 Developing and Maintaining the Handbook(s)

The QuEST Forum is responsible for the development, publication, distribution, and maintenance of the TL 9000 Handbooks that are publicly available. Change requests for the handbooks, following their initial publication, are to be submitted to the Forum Administrator. Any user of the handbooks may submit change requests. Change requests will be forwarded to the appropriate Handbook section chairperson by the Forum Administrator, and will be considered for the next revision.

Final approval of all changes to TL 9000 will be by vote of the QuEST Forum voting members in accordance with the Forum's bylaws. Re-issue of the TL 9000 Handbooks will be determined by the Forum, but not to exceed five (5) years following the last issue date. When the Forum determines there are issues in the standard that could impact third party registration, then addenda or similar communication mechanisms will be employed to inform the industry of corrections and updates to the standard.

# Section 2 - Structure

**2.1 Overall Structure**

TL 9000 is structured in layers (See Figure 1):

- International Standard - ISO 9001
- Common TL 9000 Requirements
- Hardware, Software and Services Specific Quality System Requirements
- Common TL 9000 Metrics
- Hardware, Software and Services Specific Quality System Metrics

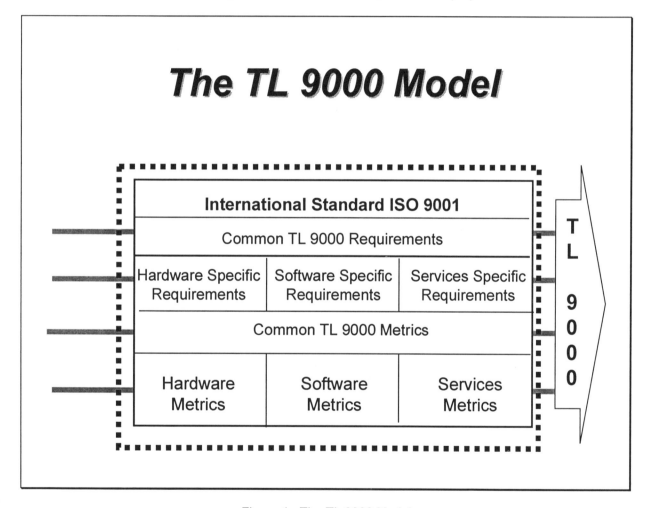

Figure 1.  The TL 9000 Model

## 2.2 Structure of Sections

ISO 9001:1994 Clause 4 has been adopted as the foundation for this Handbook.  All references to ISO 9001 are printed *in Italics* and enclosed in a text box. **For the purposes of TL 9000, the term "product," as used within the ISO 9000 series, includes hardware, software or services.**

Interpretations and supplemental quality system requirements have been harmonized and are printed in plain text.

The QuEST Forum retains full control over the content except for material that is copyrighted by others.

Section 4 "Quality System Requirements" contains the auditable requirements.  Each of the TL 9000 specific requirements is tagged with an identifier to define the related scope of that requirement.   The following table describes each of these identifiers:

| Code | Description | Example |
|------|-------------|---------|
| C | Common (H, S & V) | 4.4.4.C.1 |
| H | Hardware Only | 4.4.4.H.1 |
| HS | Hardware & Software | 4.4.4.HS.1 |
| HV | Hardware & Services | 4.4.4.HV.1 |
| S | Software Only | 4.4.4.S.1 |
| V | Services Only | 4.4.4.V.1 |
| VS | Services & Software | 4.4.4.VS.1 |

The use of terms in TL 9000 such as **shall**, **should**, **may,** and **can** follow the standard ISO definitions.  The word **shall** indicates mandatory requirements.  The word **should** indicates a preferred approach.  Suppliers choosing other approaches must be able to show that their approach meets the intent of TL 9000.  Where the words **typical** and **examples** are used, an appropriate alternative for the particular commodity or process should be chosen.

Paragraphs marked **NOTE** are for guidance and are not subject to audit.  NOTES taken directly from ISO 9001 are numbered, and these numbers begin at 5 because only notes from Section 4 are taken from ISO 9001. NOTES 1-4 are not included because they are part of ISO 9001 Section 1-3. NOTES X (alphabetical) are notes that were added by the Forum.

Endnotes denoted by **[x]** represent bibliography source material that is not auditable.

## 2.3  Terminology

The International Standard, ISO 8402:1994, *Quality Management and Quality Assurance — Vocabulary,* contains standard definitions of terms used within this handbook.  These definitions are considered part of the provisions throughout all sections of this handbook.

# Section 3 - TL 9000 Administration

## 3.1 Registration Options

The scope of a registration may apply to hardware, software, services or any combination thereof.  The TL 9000 registration may include an entire company, an organizational unit,  a facility(s), or a limited, defined product line as mutually agreed by the supplier and the registrar.  The scope of TL 9000 registration will be clearly defined within the certificate.

TL 9000 supports three distinct certifications:

| | |
|---|---|
| TL 9000-HW | Hardware |
| TL 9000-SW | Software |
| TL 9000-SC | Services |

A company may request registration to any of the above specialty areas or any combination thereof.   For example, registration of a quality system specifically for Hardware (TL 9000-HW) requires that only the requirements with identifiers Hardware (H) be addressed in addition to the ISO 9001 and Common (C) identified requirements as well as Common and Hardware Metrics.

Table 1 identifies the type of certification and the required sections in the TL 9000 Handbooks (as denoted by "X").

| Type of Certification | TL 9000 Section | | | | | | | | |
|---|---|---|---|---|---|---|---|---|---|
| | ISO (Italics) | Common Reqs. (C) | Hardware Reqs. (H) | Software Reqs. (S) | Services Reqs. (V) | Common Metrics | Hardware Metrics | Software Metrics | Services Metrics |
| Hardware only | X | X | X | | | X | X | | |
| Software only | X | X | | X | | X | | X | |
| Services only | X | X | | | X | X | | | X |

Table 1: Type of Certification

Any combination of certification types also requires conformance to their appropriate sections in the handbooks.

The method by which a supplier demonstrates conformance to the TL 9000 requirements is by successfully completing a third-party registration audit by an accredited TL 9000 registrar.  For each three (3)-year interval, 100% of the scope of the entity being registered and the TL 9000 elements shall be assessed.  For companies with mature quality systems, there are also alternative methods for maintaining registration.  These methods include third-party registrars, but leverage certain existing elements of the supplier's quality system to reduce cost and add value.  In order to use the alternative method, eligibility criteria must be satisfied.

Guidelines for alternative methods for maintaining registration are published by the International Accreditation Forum (IAF). The IAF is an international consortium of accreditation bodies. Typically, a supplier wishing to maintain registration to TL 9000 via an alternative method would first begin working with a third-party registrar to determine eligibility. See the Appendix, "Alternative Method for Maintaining TL 9000 Certification/Registration."

## 3.2 Migration Path

The QuEST Forum recognizes the achievement of existing quality system efforts. These efforts will be leveraged in the migration path to TL 9000.

Currently implemented quality systems and maturity levels are considered in the transition to TL 9000. A matrix defining the steps needed to come into compliance with the standard are included in the Appendix titled "Migration Path and Audit Days." Various schemes are described along with recommended industry compliance time frames.

## 3.3 Publicizing Registration

Members of the telecommunications industry certified by an accredited TL 9000 registrar may publicize the fact that their quality management systems have been approved for the scope identified on their registration certificates. Suppliers may not state or imply that their products are registered or certified to TL 9000. The specific rules for publicizing TL 9000 registration are as follows:

- The registered unit is entitled to use certification marks on letterheads, brochures and other promotional material;
- The mark shall not be used on manufactured product, packaging, trade samples, or other statements of Product Compliance;
- The mark shall only be used to imply that certification exists as defined in the scope of approvals stated on the certificate;
- References to the TL 9000 registration shall only apply to the scope as defined on the certificate;
- The mark shall not be used on flags, buildings, or vehicles;
- The supplier shall not publish or circulate an image of a product with TL 9000 stamped on or across it;
- In the event that certification ceases to be valid for any reason, the certificate holder shall immediately discontinue all use and distribution of any letterheads; promotional material bearing the mark, and any claims to registration;
- Misuse of the mark may be grounds for withdrawal of certification;
- Certificate holders shall abide by the requirements of the accreditation bodies and registrars that issued the certificates; and
- Products may be advertised as being produced using a TL 9000 registered quality management system.

## 3.4 (Re) Qualifying Registration Entities

The QuEST Forum establishes requirements for accreditation bodies to use in qualifying registrars. The Forum defines requirements that registrars must satisfy to carry out TL 9000 registrations; see the Appendix, "TL 9000 Accreditation Body Implementation Requirements."

Third-party registration is addressed in the Appendix, "Registration Procedures."

## 3.5 Accreditation Bodies

Accredited registrars carry out registration of a supplier's quality management system to TL 9000. Accreditation of registrars is the responsibility of accreditation bodies that are recognized by the QuEST Forum. An accreditation body is responsible for examining registrar qualifications and processes to certify that they have adequately trained and experienced personnel, necessary organizational structure and procedure(s), and other attributes as stated in the Appendix, "Code of Practice for TL 9000 Registrars." Contact the QuEST Forum Administrator for the list of recognized accreditation bodies.

## 3.6 Registrars

Registrars are responsible for verifying that the suppliers, with whom they contract to provide registration to TL 9000, have implemented a quality management system that complies with TL 9000. This responsibility is ongoing as long as the registration contract is active. In carrying out this responsibility, registrars must comply with their own procedure(s), the requirements of their contracted registrar accreditation body(ies), and with Appendix, "Code of Practice for TL 9000 Registrars". A registrar must be fully recognized by an accreditation body that is recognized by the QuEST Forum. Contact the QuEST Forum Administrator for the list of TL 9000 accredited registrars.

## 3.7 Training

The QuEST Forum is responsible for assuring the availability of appropriate training to help users correctly and consistently interpret and apply the TL 9000 requirements. All training providers that train registrars' assessors must be approved by the QuEST Forum.

# Section 4 - Quality System Requirements

## Management Responsibility - Element 4.1

**Quality Policy
4.1.1**

> The supplier's management with executive responsibility shall define and document its policy for quality, including objectives for quality and its commitment to quality. The quality policy shall be relevant to the supplier's organizational goals and the expectations and needs of its customers. The supplier shall ensure that this policy is understood, implemented, and maintained at all levels of the organization.

**4.1.1.C.1 Quality Objectives** – Objectives for quality shall include targets for the TL 9000 metrics defined in the TL 9000 Quality System Metrics handbook.

**C-NOTE A:** Management with executive responsibility should demonstrate their active involvement in long- and short-term quality planning.

**Organization
4.1.2**

> **4.1.2.1 Responsibility and Authority** - The responsibility, authority, and the interrelation of personnel who manage, perform and verify work affecting quality shall be defined and documented, particularly for personnel who need the organizational freedom and authority to:
>
> a) Initiate action to prevent the occurrence of any nonconformities relating to product, process and quality system;
> b) Identify and record any problems relating to the product, process and quality system;
> c) Initiate, recommend or provide solutions through designated channels;
> d) Verify the implementation of solutions;
> e) Control further processing, delivery or installation of nonconforming product until the deficiency or unsatisfactory condition has been corrected.

**4.1.2.2 Resources** - *The supplier shall identify resource requirements and provide adequate resources, including the assignment of trained personnel (see 4.18), for management, performance of work and verification activities including internal quality audits.*

**4.1.2.3 Management Representative** - *The supplier's management with executive responsibility shall appoint a member of the supplier's own management who, irrespective of other responsibilities, shall have defined authority for*

a) *Ensuring that a quality system is established, implemented and maintained in accordance with this International Standard, and*
b) *Reporting on the performance of the quality system to the supplier's management for review and as a basis for improvement of the quality system.*

*NOTE 5: The responsibility of a management representative may also include liaison with external parties on matters relating to the supplier's quality system.*

**Management Review 4.1.3**

*The supplier's management with executive responsibility shall review the quality system at defined intervals sufficient to ensure its continuing suitability and effectiveness in satisfying the requirements of this International Standard and the supplier's stated quality policy and objectives (see 4.1.1). Records of such reviews shall be maintained (see 4.16).*

# Quality System - Element 4.2

**General
4.2.1**

*The supplier shall establish, document, and maintain a quality system as a means of ensuring that product conforms to specified requirements. The supplier shall prepare a quality manual covering the requirements of this International Standard. The quality manual shall include or make reference to the quality-system procedures and outline the structure of the documentation used in the quality system.*

***NOTE 6:** Guidance on quality manuals is given in ISO 10013.*

**Quality System
Procedures
4.2.2**

*The supplier shall:*

*a) Prepare documented procedures consistent with the requirements of this International Standard and the supplier's stated quality policy, and*
*b) Effectively implement the quality system and its documented procedures.*

*For the purposes of this International Standard, the range and detail of the procedures that form part of the quality system depend on the complexity of the work, the methods used and the skills and training needed by personnel involved in carrying out the activity.*

***NOTE 7:** Documented procedures may make reference to work instructions that define how an activity is performed.*

**4.2.2.C.1 Life Cycle Model** - The supplier shall establish and maintain an integrated set of guidelines that covers the life cycle of its products. This framework shall contain the processes, activities, and tasks involved in the development, operation, and maintenance and (if required) disposal of products, spanning the life of the products. [9]

**4.2.2.S.1 Support Software and Tools Management** - The supplier shall ensure that internally developed support software and tools used in the product life cycle are subject to the appropriate quality method(s). Tools to be considered include: design and development tools, testing tools, configuration management tools, and documentation tools. [10]

**Quality Planning
4.2.3**

*The supplier shall define and document how the requirements for quality will be met. Quality planning shall be consistent with all other requirements of a supplier's quality system and shall be documented in a format to suit the supplier's method of operation. The supplier shall give consideration to the following activities, as appropriate, in meeting the specified requirements for products, projects, or contracts:*

*a) The preparation of quality plans;*
*b) The identification and acquisition of any controls, processes, equipment (including inspection and test equipment), fixtures, resources and skills that may be needed to achieve the required quality;*
*c) Ensuring the compatibility of the design, the production process, installation, servicing, inspection, and test procedures, and the applicable documentation;*
*d) The updating, as necessary, of quality control, inspection, and testing techniques, including the development of new instrumentation;*
*e) The identification of any measurement requirement involving capability that exceeds the known state of the art, in sufficient time for the needed capability to be developed;*
*f) The identification of suitable verification at appropriate stages in the realization of product;*
*g) The clarification of standards of acceptability for all features and requirements, including those which contain a subjective element;*
*h) The identification and preparation of quality records (see 4.16).*

**NOTE 8:** *The quality plans referred to (see 4.2.3a) may be in the form of a reference to the appropriate documented procedures that form an integral part of the supplier's quality system.*

**4.2.3.C.1 Customer Involvement** - The supplier shall establish and maintain methods for soliciting and considering customer input for quality planning activities. Consideration should be given to establishing joint customer-supplier quality improvement programs. [4]

**4.2.3.C.2 Long- and Short-Term Planning** - The supplier's quality planning activities shall include long- and short-term plans with goals for improving quality and customer satisfaction. These plans shall address:

a) Cycle time;
b) Customer service;
c) Training;
d) Cost;
e) Delivery commitments; and
f) Product reliability.

Performance to these goals shall be monitored and reported.

**4.2.3.C.3 Subcontractor Input** - The supplier shall establish and maintain methods for soliciting and using subcontractor input for quality planning activities. [4]

**4.2.3.C.4 Disaster Recovery** - The supplier shall establish and maintain methods for disaster recovery to ensure the ability to recreate and service the product throughout its life cycle. [9]

## Contract Review - Element 4.3

**General**
**4.3.1**

> The supplier shall establish and maintain documented procedures for contract review and for the coordination of these activities.

**Review**
**4.3.2**

> Before submission of a tender, or at the acceptance of a contract or order (statement of requirement), the tender, contract or order shall be reviewed by the supplier to ensure that:
>
> a) The requirements are adequately defined and documented; where no written statement or requirement is available for an order received by verbal means, the supplier shall ensure that the order requirements are agreed before their acceptance;
> b) Any differences between the contract or accepted order requirements and those in the tender are resolved;
> c) The supplier has the capability to meet the contract or accepted order requirements.

**C-NOTE B:** The contract review process should include:
a) Product acceptance planning and review;
b) Handling of problems detected after product acceptance, including customer complaints and claims; and
c) Responsibility of removal and/or correction of nonconformities after applicable warranty period or during product maintenance contract period. [8]

**C-NOTE C:** The product acceptance plan should include as appropriate:
a) Acceptance review process;
b) Acceptance criteria;
c) Documented test procedure(s);
d) Test environment;
e) Test cases;
f) Test data;
g) Resources involved;
h) Method(s) for problem tracking and resolution; and
i) Required acceptance test reports. [9]

**Amendment**
**to Contract**
**4.3.3**

> The supplier shall identify how an amendment to a contract is made and correctly transferred to the functions concerned within the supplier's organization.

**Records
4.3.4**

Records of contract reviews shall be maintained (see 4.16).

**NOTE 9:** Channels for communication and interfaces with the customer's organization in these contract matters should be established.

# Design Control - Element 4.4

| | |
|---|---|
| **General**<br>**4.4.1** | *The supplier shall establish and maintain documented procedures to control and verify the design of the product in order to ensure that the specified requirements are met.* |

**V-NOTE D: Design of Services** – All design control requirements apply to suppliers that are responsible for the design of delivered services.

**4.4.1.C.1 Requirements Traceability** - The supplier shall establish and maintain a method to trace specified requirements through design and test. [10]

| | |
|---|---|
| **Design and**<br>**Development**<br>**Planning**<br>**4.4.2** | *The supplier shall prepare plans for each design and development activity. The plans shall describe or reference these activities, and define responsibility for their implementation. The design and development activities shall be assigned to qualified personnel equipped with adequate resources. The plans shall be updated, as the design evolves.* |

**4.4.2.C.1 Project Plan** - The supplier shall establish and maintain a project plan based upon the defined product life cycle model. The plan should include:
a) Project organizational structure;
b) Project roles and responsibilities;
c) Interfaces with internal and external organizations;
d) Means for scheduling, tracking, issue resolution, and reporting;
e) Budgets, staffing, and schedules associated with project activities;
f) Method(s), standards, documented procedure(s), and tools to be used;
g) References to related plans (e.g., development, testing, configuration management, and quality);
h) Project-specific environment and physical resource considerations (e.g., development, user documentation, testing, and operation);
i) Customer, user, and subcontractor involvement during the product life cycle (e.g., joint reviews, informal meetings, and approvals);
j) Management of project quality;
k) Risk management and contingency plans (e.g., technical, cost and schedules);
l) Performance, safety, security, and other critical requirements;
m) Project-specific training requirements;
n) Required certifications;
o) Proprietary, usage, ownership, warranty and licensing rights; and
p) Post-project analysis. [9]

**C-NOTE E:** The project plan and any related plans may be an independent document, a part of another document, or composed of several documents.

**C-NOTE F:** General work instructions defining tasks and responsibilities common to all development projects need not be replicated as part of a documented project plan.

**4.4.2.C.2 Test Planning** - Test plans shall be documented and results recorded. Test plans should include:
a) Scope of testing (e.g., unit, feature, integration, system, acceptance);
b) Types of tests to be performed (e.g., functional, boundary, usability, performance, regression, interoperability);
c) Traceability to requirements;
d) Test environment (e.g., relevancy to customer environment, operational use);
e) Test coverage;
f) Expected results;
g) Data definition and database requirements;
h) Set of tests, test cases (inputs, outputs, test criteria), and documented test procedure(s); and
i) Use of external testing. [10]

**C-NOTE G:** Testing may be covered at several levels.

**4.4.2.C.3 End of Life Planning** - The supplier shall establish and maintain a documented procedure(s) for the discontinuance of manufacturing and/or support of a product by the operation and service organizations. This documented procedure(s) should include:
a) Cessation of full or partial support after a certain period of time;
b) Archiving product documentation and software;
c) Responsibility for any future residual support issues;
d) Transition to the new product, if applicable; and
e) Accessibility of archive copies of data. [9]

**4.4.2.S.1 Estimation** - The supplier shall establish and maintain a method for estimating and tracking project factors during project planning, execution, and change management. Project factors to be considered should include product size, complexity, effort, staffing, schedules, cost, quality, reliability, and productivity. [10]

**4.4.2.S.2 Computer Resources** - The supplier shall establish and maintain methods for estimating and tracking critical computer resources for the target computer. Examples of these resources are utilization of memory, throughput, real time performance, and I/O channels. [10]

**4.4.2.S.3 Integration Planning** – The supplier shall develop and document a plan to integrate the software components into the product. The plan shall include:
a) Methods and documented procedure(s);
b) Responsibilities;
c) Schedule for integration; and
d) Test requirements. [9]

**4.4.2.S.4 Migration Planning** - When a system or software product is planned to be migrated from an old to a new environment, the supplier shall develop and document a migration plan. This plan should include the following:
a) Requirements analysis and definition of migration;

b)   Development of migration tools;
c)   Conversion of product and data;
d)   Migration execution;
e)   Migration verification; and
f)   Support for the old environment in the future. [9]

### Organizational and Technical Interfaces 4.4.3

*Organizational and technical interfaces between different groups which input into the design process shall be defined and the necessary information documented, transmitted, and regularly reviewed.*

**C-NOTE H:**  The supplier should establish communication methods for dissemination of product requirements, and changes to requirements to all impacted parties identified in the project plan.

### Design Input 4.4.4

*Design-input requirements relating to the product, including applicable statutory and regulatory requirements, shall be identified, documented and their selection reviewed by the supplier for adequacy.  Incomplete, ambiguous, or conflicting requirements shall be resolved with those responsible for imposing these requirements.*

*Design input shall take into consideration the results of any contract-review activities.*

**4.4.4.C.1  Customer and Subcontractor Input** - The supplier shall establish and maintain methods for soliciting and using customer and  subcontractor input during the development of new or revised product requirements. [4]

**4.4.4.C.2  Design Requirements** - Design requirements shall be defined and documented, and should include:
a)   Quality and reliability requirements;
b)   Functions and capabilities of the product;
c)   Business, organizational, and user requirements;
d)   Safety, environmental, and security requirements;
e)   Installability, usability and maintainability requirements;
f)   Design constraints; and
g)   Testing requirements. [9]

**4.4.4.H.1  Content of Requirements** - The design requirements shall include, but are not limited to:
a)   Nominal values and tolerances;
b)   Maintainability needs; and
c)   End item packaging requirements. [5]

**4.4.4.S.1 Identification of Software Requirements** - The supplier shall determine, analyze, and document the software component requirements of the system.[9]

**4.4.4.S.2 Requirements Allocation** - The supplier shall document the allocation of the product requirements to the product architecture.[8]

---

**Design Output
4.4.5**

> *Design output shall be documented and expressed in terms that can be verified against design-input requirements and validated (see 4.4.8).*
>
> *Design output shall:*
>
> a) *Meet the design-input requirements;*
> b) *Contain or make reference to acceptance criteria;*
> c) *Identify those characteristics of the design that are crucial to the safe and proper functioning of the product (e.g., operating, storage, handling, maintenance and disposal requirements).*
>
> *Design-output documents shall be reviewed before release.*

**4.4.5.S.1 Design Output** - The required output from the design activity shall be defined and documented in accordance with the chosen method. Design outputs may include, but are not limited to:
a) Architectural design;
b) Detailed design;
c) Source code; and
d) User documentation. [8]

**4.4.5.V.1 Services Design Output** - The required output from the services design shall contain a complete and precise statement of the service to be provided. Design outputs shall include, but are not limited to:
a) Service delivery procedures;
b) Resource and skill requirements;
c) Reliance on sub-contractors;
d) Service characteristics subject to customer evaluation; and
e) Standards of acceptability for each service characteristic.[12]

---

**Design Review
4.4.6**

> *At appropriate stages of design, formal documented reviews of the design results shall be planned and conducted. Participants at each design review shall include representatives of all functions concerned with the design stage being reviewed, as well as other specialist personnel, as required. Records of such reviews shall be maintained (see 4.16).*

**Design
Verification
4.4.7**

At appropriate stages of design, design verification shall be performed to ensure that the design-stage output meets the design-stage input requirements. The design-verification measures shall be recorded (see 4.16).

*NOTE 10:* In addition to conducting design reviews (see 4.4.6), design verification may include activities such as:

- Performing alternative calculations,
- Comparing the new design with a similar proven design, if available,
- Undertaking tests and demonstrations, and
- Reviewing the design-stage documents before release.

**C-NOTE I:** See 4.10 for related requirements.

**Design Validation
4.4.8**

Design validation shall be performed to ensure that product conforms to defined user needs and/or requirements.

*NOTE 11:* Design validation follows successful design verification (see 4.4.7).
*NOTE 12:* Validation is normally performed under defined operating conditions.
*NOTE 13:* Validation is normally performed on the final product, but may be necessary in earlier stages prior to product completion.
*NOTE 14:* Multiple validations may be performed if there are different intended uses.

**HV-NOTE J:** See 4.10 for related requirements.

**C-NOTE K:** It may be beneficial to include customers or a third party during various validation stages.

**4.4.8.H.1 Periodic Retesting** - The supplier shall establish and maintain a documented procedure(s) that ensures products are periodically retested to assess the product's ability to continue to meet design requirements. [5]

**4.4.8.H.2 Content of Testing** - The initial test and periodic retest shall be more extensive than the routine quality control tests. The initial test shall include those that are contained in the customer and/or supplier product specifications and/or contracts. The results of these tests shall be documented (See 4.16). [5]

**H-NOTE L:** Product specifications may include environmental, vibration, flammability, and operational stress type testing.

**4.4.8.H.3 Frequency of Testing** - The supplier shall establish and document the frequency for test/periodic retest. When determining the test frequency, the supplier shall include the following:
a) Product complexity and service criticality;

b) Number of design, engineering and/or manufacturing changes made to the product and whether the change(s) affect form, fit, and/or function;
c) Changes to the manufacturing process;
d) Manufacturing variations, (e.g., tooling wear);
e) Material and/or component substitutions and failure rates; and
f) The field performance record of the product. [5]

**Design Changes**
**4.4.9**

All design changes and modifications shall be identified, documented, reviewed and approved by authorized personnel before their implementation.

**4.4.9.C.1 Change Management Process** - The supplier shall establish and maintain a process to ensure that all requirements and design changes, which may arise at any time during the product life cycle, are managed in a systematic and timely manner and do not adversely affect quality and reliability. Management of changes should include:
a) Impact analysis;
b) Planning;
c) Implementation;
d) Testing;
e) Documentation;
f) Communication; and
g) Review and approval. [5]

**4.4.9.C.2 Informing Customers** - The supplier shall establish and maintain a documented procedure(s) to ensure that customers are informed when design changes effect contractual commitments. [5]

**4.4.9.H.1 Tracking of Changes** - The supplier shall track design changes and shall use the results to ensure that the product still fulfills its design intent. [5]

**4.4.9.H.2 Component Changes** - The supplier shall have adequate documented procedure(s) in place to ensure that material or component substitutions or changes do not adversely affect product quality or performance.

**H-NOTE M:** These documented procedure(s) should include:
a) Functional testing;
b) Qualification testing;
c) Stress testing;
d) Approved parts listing; and/or
e) Critical parts listing.

**4.4.9.V.1 Tool Changes** – The supplier shall have documented procedure(s) in place to ensure that substitutions or changes to tools used in performing the service do not adversely affect the quality of the service.

# Document and Data Control - Element 4.5

**General**
**4.5.1**

*The supplier shall establish and maintain documented procedures to control all documents and data that relate to the requirements of this International Standard including, to the extent applicable, documents of external origin such as standards and customer drawings.*

*NOTE 15: Documents and data can be in the form of any type of media, such as hard copy or electronic media.*

**4.5.1.S.1  Control of Customer-Supplied Documents and Data** –The supplier shall establish and maintain documented procedure(s) to control all customer-supplied documents and data (e.g., network architecture, topology, capacity, and database) if these documents and data influence the design, verification, validation, inspection and testing, or servicing the product.

**Document and Data Approval and Issue**
**4.5.2**

*The documents and data shall be reviewed and approved for adequacy by authorized personnel prior to issue. A master list or equivalent document-control procedure identifying the current revision status of documents shall be established and be readily available to preclude the use of invalid and/or obsolete documents.*

*This control shall ensure that:*

a)   *The pertinent issues of appropriate documents are available at all locations where operations essential to the effective functioning of the quality system are performed;*
b)   *Invalid and/or obsolete documents are promptly removed from all points of issue or use, or otherwise assured against unintended use;*
c)   *Any obsolete documents retained for legal and/or knowledge-preservation purposes are suitably identified.*

**Document and
Data Changes
4.5.3**

*Changes to documents and data shall be reviewed and approved by the same functions/organizations that performed the original review and approval, unless specifically designated otherwise. The designated functions/organizations shall have access to pertinent background information upon which to base their review and approval.*

*Where practicable, the nature of the change shall be identified in the document or the appropriate attachments.*

## Purchasing - Element 4.6

| | |
|---|---|
| **General**<br>**4.6.1** | *The supplier shall establish and maintain documented procedures to ensure that purchased product (see 3.1) conforms to specified requirements.* |

**C-NOTE N:** The reference to "(see 3.1)" above references ISO 9001:1994, which is not included in this document.

**4.6.1.C.1 Purchasing Procedure(s)** - The documented purchasing procedure(s) shall include:
a) Product requirements definition;
b) Risk analysis and management;
c) Qualification criteria;
d) Contract definition;
e) Proprietary, usage, ownership, warranty and licensing rights are satisfied;
f) Future support for the product is planned;
g) Ongoing supply-base management and monitoring;
h) Subcontractor selection criteria; and
i) Subcontractor re-evaluation;
j) Feedback to key subcontractors based on data analysis of subcontractor performance.[9]

**C-NOTE O:** This documented procedure(s) should be applicable to off-the-shelf product. This typically includes original equipment manufacturer (OEM) products used in manufacturing and commercial off-the-shelf (COTS) products used in software systems.

| | |
|---|---|
| **Evaluation of**<br>**Subcontractors**<br>**4.6.2** | *The supplier shall:*<br><br>a) *Evaluate and select subcontractors on the basis of their ability to meet subcontract requirements including the quality system and any specific quality-assurance requirements;*<br>b) *Define the type and extent of control exercised by the supplier over subcontractors. This shall be dependent upon the type of product, the impact of subcontracted product on the quality of final product, and where applicable, on the quality audit reports and/or quality records of the previously demonstrated capability and performance of subcontractors;*<br>c) *Establish and maintain quality records of acceptable subcontractors (see 4.16).* |

**Purchasing Data
4.6.3**

*Purchasing documents shall contain data clearly describing the product ordered, including where applicable:*

a) *The type, class, grade or other precise identification;*
b) *The title or other positive identification, and applicable issues of specifications, drawings, process requirements, inspection instructions and other relevant technical data, including requirements for approval or qualification of product, procedures, process equipment, and personnel;*
c) *The title, number, and issue of the quality-system standard to be applied.*

*The supplier shall review and approve purchasing documents for adequacy of the specified requirements prior to release.*

**Verification of
Purchased
Product
4.6.4**

**4.6.4.1 Supplier Verification at Subcontractor's Premises** - *Where the supplier proposes to verify purchased product at the subcontractor's premises, the supplier shall specify verification arrangements and the method of product release in the purchasing documents.*

**4.6.4.2 Customer Verification of Subcontracted Product** - *Where specified in the contract, the supplier's customer or the customer's representative shall be afforded the right to verify at the subcontractor's premises and the supplier's premises that subcontracted product conforms to specified requirements. Such verification shall not be used by the supplier as evidence of effective control of quality by the subcontractor.*

*Verification by the customer shall not absolve the supplier of the responsibility to provide acceptable product, nor shall it preclude subsequent rejection by the customer.*

## Control of Customer-Supplied Product - Element 4.7

> *The supplier shall establish and maintain documented procedures for the control of verification, storage, and maintenance of customer-supplied product provided for incorporation into the supplies or for related activities. Any such product that is lost, damaged, or is otherwise unsuitable for use shall be recorded and reported to the customer (see 4.16).*
>
> *Verification by the supplier does not absolve the customer of the responsibility to provide acceptable product.*

## Product Identification and Traceability - Element 4.8

> *Where appropriate, the supplier shall establish and maintain documented procedures for identifying the product by suitable means from receipt and during all stages of production, delivery, and installation.*
>
> *Where and to the extent that traceability is a specified requirement, the supplier shall establish and maintain documented procedures for unique identification of individual product or batches. This identification shall be recorded (see 4.16).*

**4.8.H.1 Traceability for Recall** - Field Replaceable Units (FRU) shall be traceable throughout the product life cycle in a way that helps suppliers and customers to identify products being recalled, needing to be replaced or modified.

**4.8.H.2 Traceability of Design Changes** – The supplier shall establish and maintain documented procedure(s) which provide traceability of design changes to identifiable manufacturing dates, lots, or serial numbers.

**4.8.HS.1 Configuration Management Plan** - The supplier shall establish and maintain a configuration management plan which should include:
a) Identification and scope of the configuration management activities;
b) Schedule for performing these activities;
c) Configuration management tools;
d) Configuration management methods and documented procedure(s);
e) Organizations and responsibilities assigned to them;
f) Level of required control for each configuration item; and
g) Point at which items are brought under configuration management. [9]

**HS-NOTE P:** General work instructions defining general configuration management tasks and responsibilities need not be replicated as part of a specific documented configuration management plan.

**4.8.HS.2 Product Identification** - The supplier shall establish and maintain a process for the identification of each product and the level of required control. For each product and its versions, the following shall be identified as appropriate:
a) Documentation;
b) Associated tools needed for product re-creation;
c) Interfaces to other software and hardware; and
d) Software and hardware environment. [8]

# Process Control - Element 4.9

The supplier shall identify and plan the production, installation, and servicing processes which directly affect quality and shall ensure that these processes are carried out under controlled conditions. Controlled conditions shall include the following:

a) Documented procedures defining the manner of production, installation, and servicing, where the absence of such procedures could adversely affect quality;

b) Use of suitable production, installation, and servicing equipment and a suitable working environment;

c) Compliance with reference standards/codes, quality plans and/or documented procedures;

d) Monitoring and control of suitable process parameters and product characteristics;

e) The approval of processes and equipment, as appropriate;

f) Criteria for workmanship, which shall be stipulated in the clearest practical manner (e.g., written standards, representative samples or illustrations);

g) Suitable maintenance of equipment to ensure continuing process capability.

Where the results of processes cannot be fully verified by subsequent inspection and testing of the product and where, for example, processing deficiencies may become apparent only after the product is in use, the processes shall be carried out by qualified operators and/or shall require continuous monitoring and control of process parameters to ensure that the specified requirements are met.

The requirements for any qualification of process operations, including associated equipment and personnel (see 4.18), shall be specified.

**NOTE 16:** Such processes requiring pre-qualification of their process capability are frequently referred to as special processes.

Records shall be maintained for qualified processes, equipment and personnel, as appropriate (see 4.16).

**4.9.H.1 Inspection and Testing** - Inspection and testing results shall be recorded and analyzed for the purpose of identifying problem areas. [5]

**4.9.HV.1 Operational Changes** - Each time a significant change is made in the established operation (e.g., a new operator, new machine, or new technique), a critical examination shall be made of the first unit(s)/service(s) processed after the change. [5]

**4.9.HV.2 Operator Qualification** - The supplier shall establish operator qualification and requalification requirements for all applicable processes. These requirements, as a minimum, shall address employee experience, training, and demonstrated skills. The supplier shall communicate this information to all affected employees. [4]

**4.9.HV.3 Employee Skills List** - The supplier shall maintain records of employees and their skills and qualifications (e.g., employee skills bank or training records) to aid in determination of work assignments. [4]

**4.9.S.1 Replication** - The supplier shall establish and maintain a documented procedure(s) for replication which should include the following:
a)  Identification of the master copy and copies to be delivered;
b)  The number of copies to be delivered;
c)  Type of media and associated labeling;
d)  Identification and packaging of required documentation such as user manuals; and
e)  Controlling the replication environment to ensure repeatability. [8]

**4.9.S.2 Release Management** – The supplier shall establish and maintain documented procedure(s) to control the release and delivery of software products and documentation. These documented procedure(s) should include methods to provide for the following:
a)  Release planning information delivered to the customer sufficiently in advance of the release;
b)  Product introduction and release schedules to the customer;
c)  Detailed descriptions of product features delivered, and changes incorporated in new software products or releases; and
d)  Advising the customer of current or planned changes. [10]

**4.9.V.1 Software Used in Service Delivery** - Suppliers shall document and implement processes for the maintenance and control of software used in service delivery to ensure continued process capability and integrity.

**4.9.V.2 Service Delivery Plan** – Suppliers that are responsible for the delivery or implementation of a service, and are not responsible for the design of that service, shall comply with the Project Plan requirements of 4.4.2.C.1.

# nspection and Testing - Element 4.10

**General**
**4.10.1**

> The supplier shall establish and maintain documented procedures for inspection and testing activities in order to verify that the specified requirements for the product are met. The required inspection and testing, and the records to be established, shall be detailed in the quality plan or documented procedures.

**C-NOTE Q:** See 4.4.7 and 4.4.8 for related requirements.

**4.10.1.HV.1 Inspection and Test Documentation** - Each inspection or testing activity shall have detailed documentation. Details should include the following:
a) Parameters to be checked with acceptable tolerances;
b) The use of statistical techniques, control charts, etc.;
c) Sampling plan, including frequency, sample size, and acceptance criteria;
d) Handling of nonconformances;
e) Data to be recorded;
f) Defect classification scheme;
g) Method for designating an inspection item or lot; and
h) Electrical, functional, and feature testing. [5]

**4.10.1.S.1 Test Documentation** - Software tests shall be conducted according to documented procedure(s) and the test plan. Documentation of testing shall include:
a) Test results;
b) Analysis of test results;
c) Conformance to expected results; and
d) Problem reporting for nonconforming items. [10]

**Receiving**
**Inspection and**
**Testing**
**4.10.2**

> **4.10.2.1** The supplier shall ensure that incoming product is not used or processed (except in the circumstances described in 4.10.2.3) until it has been inspected or otherwise verified as conforming to specified requirements. Verification of the specified requirements shall be in accordance with the quality plan and/or documented procedures.

> **4.10.2.2** In determining the amount and nature of receiving inspection, consideration shall be given to the amount of control exercised at the subcontractor's premises and the recorded evidence of conformance provided.

*4.10.2.3 Where incoming product is released for urgent production purposes prior to verification, it shall be positively identified and recorded (see 4.16) in order to permit immediate recall and replacement in the event of nonconformity to specified requirements.*

## In Process Inspection and Testing 4.10.3

*The supplier shall:*

*a) Inspect and test the product as required by the quality plan and/or documented procedures;*
*b) Hold product until the required inspection and tests have been completed or necessary reports have been received and verified, except when product is released under positive-recall procedures (see 4.10.2.3). Release under positive-recall procedures shall not preclude the activities outlined in 4.10.3a.*

## Final Inspection and Testing 4.10.4

*The supplier shall carry out all final inspection and testing in accordance with the quality plan and/or documented procedures to complete the evidence of conformance of the finished product to the specified requirements.*

*The quality plan and/or documented procedures for final inspection and testing shall require that all specified inspection and tests, including those specified either on receipt of product or in-process, have been carried out and that the results meet specified requirements.*

*No product shall be dispatched until all the activities specified in the quality plan and/or documented procedures have been satisfactorily completed and the associated data and documentation are available and authorized.*

**4.10.4.H.1 Testing of Repair and Return Products** - Repair and return products shall be subjected to the same or equivalent documented final acceptance test procedure(s) as newly manufactured products.[5]

**4.10.4.H.2 Packaging and Labeling Audit** - The supplier shall include a packaging and labeling audit in the quality plan or documented procedure(s). This may include, for example, marking, labeling, kiting, documentation, customer-specific marking, and correct quantities.

**H-NOTE R:** This audit is normally done on products ready to ship.

**Inspection and
Test Records
4.10.5**

*The supplier shall establish and maintain records which provide evidence that the product has been inspected and/or tested. These records shall show clearly whether the product has passed or failed the inspections and/or tests according to defined acceptance criteria. Where the product fails to pass any inspections and/or test, the procedures for control of nonconforming product shall apply (see 4.13).*

*Records shall identify the inspection authority responsible for the release of product (see 4.16).*

**4.10.5.HV.1 Inspection and Test Records** - Inspection and test records shall include:
a) Product identification;
b) Quantity of product inspected;
c) Documented inspection procedure(s) followed;
d) Person performing the test and inspection;
e) Date of inspection and/or test; and
f) Number, type, and severity of defects found." [5]

## Control of Inspection, Measuring, and Test Equipment - Element 4.11

| | |
|---|---|
| **General 4.11.1** | The supplier shall establish and maintain documented procedures to control, calibrate, and maintain inspection, measuring, and test equipment (including test software) used by the supplier to demonstrate the conformance of product to the specified requirements. Inspection, measuring, and test equipment shall be used in a manner which ensures that the measurement uncertainty is known and is consistent with the required measurement capability.

Where test software or comparative references such as test hardware are used as suitable forms of inspection, they shall be checked to prove that they are capable of verifying the acceptability of product, prior to release for use during production, installation, or servicing, and shall be rechecked at prescribed intervals. The supplier shall establish the extent and frequency of such checks and shall maintain records as evidence of control (see 4.16).

Where the availability of technical data pertaining to the measurement equipment is a specified requirement, such data shall be made available, when required by the customer or customer's representative, for verification that the measuring equipment is functionally adequate.

**NOTE 17:** For the purposes of this International Standard, the term "measuring equipment" includes measurement devices. |

| | |
|---|---|
| **Control Procedure 4.11.2** | The supplier shall:

a)  Determine the measurements to be made and the accuracy required, and select the appropriate inspection, measuring, and test equipment that is capable of the necessary accuracy and precision;
b)  Identify all inspection, measuring, and test equipment that can affect product quality, and calibrate and adjust them at prescribed intervals, or prior to use, against certified equipment having a known valid relationship to internationally or nationally recognized standards.  Where no such standards exist, the basis used for calibration shall be documented;
c)  Define the process employed for the calibration of inspection, measuring, and test equipment, including details of equipment type, unique identification, location, frequency of checks, check method, acceptance criteria, and the action to be taken when results are unsatisfactory;
d)  Identify inspection, measuring, and test equipment with a suitable indicator or approved identification record to show the calibration status;
e)  Maintain calibration records for inspection, measuring, and test equipment (see 4.16);
f)  Assess and document the validity of previous inspection and test results when inspection, measuring and  test equipment is found to be out of calibration; |

g)  Ensure that the environmental conditions are suitable for the calibrations, inspections, measurements and tests being carried out;

h)  Ensure that the handling, preservation and storage of inspection, measuring and test equipment is such that the accuracy and fitness for use are maintained;

i)  Safeguard inspection, measuring, and test facilities, including both test hardware and test software, from adjustments which would invalidate the calibration setting.

NOTE 18:  The metrological confirmation system for measuring equipment given in ISO 10012 may be used for guidance.

**4.11.2.H.1  Identified Equipment** - Inspection, measuring, and test equipment that is either inactive or unsuitable for use shall be identified and not used for production.  All inspection, measuring, and test equipment that does not require calibration shall be identified. [5]

## *Inspection and Test Status - Element 4.12*

*The inspection and test status of product shall be identified by suitable means, which indicate the conformance or nonconformance of product with regard to inspection and tests performed. The identification of inspection and test status shall be maintained, as defined in the quality plan and/or documented procedures, throughout production, installation, and servicing of the product to ensure that only product that has passed the required inspections and tests [or released under an authorized concession (see 4.13.2) is dispatched, used or installed.*

# Control of Nonconforming Product - Element 4.13

**General**
**4.13.1**

*The supplier shall establish and maintain documented procedures to ensure that product that does not conform to specified requirements is prevented from unintended use or installation. This control shall provide for identification, documentation, evaluation, segregation (when practical), disposition of nonconforming product and for notification to the functions concerned.*

**Review and Disposition of Nonconforming Product**
**4.13.2**

*The responsibility for review and authority for the disposition of nonconforming product shall be defined.*

*Nonconforming product shall be reviewed in accordance with documented procedures. It may be*

a) *Reworked to meet the specified requirements,*
b) *Accepted with or without repair by concession,*
c) *Regraded for alternative applications, or*
d) *Rejected or scrapped.*

*Where required by the contract, the proposed use or repair of product (see 4.13.2b) which does not conform to specified requirements shall be reported for concession to the customer or customer's representative. The description of nonconformity that has been accepted, and of repairs, shall be recorded to denote the actual condition (see 4.16).*

*Repaired and/or reworked product shall be re-inspected in accordance with the quality plan and/or documented procedures.*

**4.13.2.C.1 Trend Analysis** - Trend analysis of discrepancies found in nonconforming product shall be performed on a defined, regular basis and results utilized as input for corrective and preventive action.

## Corrective and Preventive Action - Element 4.14

**General
4.14.1**

> The supplier shall establish and maintain documented procedures for implementing corrective and preventive action.
>
> Any corrective or preventive action taken to eliminate the causes of actual or potential nonconformities shall be to a degree appropriate to the magnitude of problems and commensurate with the risks encountered.
>
> The supplier shall implement and record any changes to the documented procedures resulting from corrective and preventive action.

**C-NOTE S:** Consideration should be given to include training as part of implementing corrective and preventive actions.

**Corrective Action
4.14.2**

> The procedures for corrective action shall include:
>
> a) The effective handling of customer complaints and reports of product nonconformities;
> b) Investigation of the cause of nonconformities relating to product, process, and quality system, and recording the results of the investigation (see 4.16);
> c) Determination of the corrective action needed to eliminate the cause of nonconformities;
> d) Application of controls to ensure that corrective action is taken and that it is effective.

**C-NOTE T:** Negative deviations from plans are considered nonconformances.

**C-NOTE U:** Effective corrective action ensures that additional problems have not been introduced.

## Preventive Action
## 4.14.3

The procedures for preventive action shall include:

a) The use of appropriate sources of information such as processes and work operations which affect product quality, concessions, audit results, quality records, service reports, and customer complaints to detect, analyze, and eliminate potential causes of nonconformities;
b) Determination of the steps needed to deal with any problems requiring preventive action;
c) Initiation of preventive action and application of controls to ensure that it is effective;
d) Confirmation that relevant information on actions taken is submitted for management review (see 4.1.3).

## *Handling, Storage, Packaging, Preservation & Delivery - Element 4.15*

**General
4.15.1**

> *The supplier shall establish and maintain documented procedures for handling, storage, packaging, preservation, and delivery of product.*

**4.15.1.C.1  Work Areas** - Areas used for handling, storage, and packaging of products shall be clean, safe, and organized to ensure that they do not adversely affect quality or personnel performance. [5]

**4.15.1.C.2  Anti-Static Protection** - Anti-static protection shall be employed where applicable for components and products susceptible to electrostatic discharge (ESD) damage. Consider components and products such as: integrated circuits, printed wiring board assemblies, magnetic tapes and/or disks, and other media used for software or data storage. [5]

**Handling
4.15.2**

> *The supplier shall provide methods of handling product that prevent damage or deterioration.*

**4.15.2.S.1  Software Virus Protection** - The supplier shall establish and maintain methods for software virus prevention, detection, and removal from the deliverable product. [8]

**Storage
4.15.3**

> *The supplier shall use designated storage areas or stock rooms to prevent damage or deterioration of product, pending use or delivery. Appropriate methods for authorizing receipt to and dispatch from such areas shall be stipulated.*
>
> *In order to detect deterioration, the condition of product in stock shall be assessed at appropriate intervals.*

**4.15.3.H.1 Deterioration** - Where the possibility of deterioration exists, materials in storage shall be controlled (i.e., date stamped/coded) and materials with expired dates shall not be used. [5]

**Packaging
4.15.4**

> *The supplier shall control packing, packaging, and marking processes (including materials used) to the extent necessary to ensure conformance to specified requirements.*

**Preservation
4.15.5**

> *The supplier shall apply appropriate methods for preservation and segregation of product when the product is under the supplier's control.*

**Delivery
4.15.6**

> *The supplier shall arrange for the protection of the quality of product after final inspection and test. Where contractually specified, this protection shall be extended to include delivery to destination.*

**4.15.6.S.1 Patch Documentation** - The supplier shall establish and maintain methods to ensure that all documentation required to describe, test, install, and apply a patch has been verified and delivered with the patch. [10]

## Control of Quality Records - Element 4.16

*The supplier shall establish and maintain documented procedures for identification, collection, indexing, access, filing, storage, maintenance, and disposition of quality records.*

*Quality records shall be maintained to demonstrate conformance to specified requirements and the effective operation of the quality system. Pertinent quality records from the subcontractor shall be an element of these data.*

*All quality records shall be legible and shall be stored and retained in such a way that they are readily retrievable in facilities that provide a suitable environment to prevent damage or deterioration and to prevent loss. Retention times of quality records shall be established and recorded. Where agreed contractually, quality records shall be made available for evaluation by the customer or the customer's representative for an agreed period.*

*NOTE 19: Records may be in the form of any type of media, such as hard copy or electronic media.*

# nternal Quality Audits - Element 4.17

*The supplier shall establish and maintain documented procedures for planning and implementing internal quality audits to verify whether quality activities and related results comply with planned arrangements and to determine the effectiveness of the quality system.*

*Internal quality audits shall be scheduled on the basis of the status and importance of the activity to be audited and shall be carried out by personnel independent of those having direct responsibility for the activity being audited.*

*The results of the audits shall be recorded (see 4.16) and brought to the attention of the personnel having responsibility in the area audited. The management personnel responsible for the area shall take timely corrective action on deficiencies found during the audit.*

*Follow-up audit activities shall verify and record the implementation and effectiveness of the corrective action taken (see 4.16).*

***NOTE 20****: The results of internal quality audits form an integral part of the input to management review activities (see 4.1.3).*

***NOTE 21****: Guidance on quality-system audits is given in ANSI/ASQC Q10011-1-1994, ANSI/ASQC Q10011-2-1994, AND ANSI/ASQC Q10011-3-1994.*

## Training - Element 4.18

> *The supplier shall establish and maintain documented procedures for identifying training needs and provide for the training of all personnel performing activities affecting quality. Personnel performing specific assigned tasks shall be qualified on the basis of appropriate education, training and/or experience, as required. Appropriate records of training shall be maintained (see 4.16).*

**4.18.C.1  Course Development** – The supplier shall establish and maintain a process for planning, developing and implementing internally developed training courses. [4]

**4.18.C.2  Quality Improvement Concepts** - Those employees that have a direct impact on the quality of the product, including management with executive responsibility, shall be trained in the fundamental concepts of quality improvement, problem solving, and customer satisfaction. [4]

**4.18.C.3 Training Requirements and Awareness** - Training requirements shall be defined for all positions that have a direct  impact on the quality of products. Employees shall be made aware of training opportunities. [4]

**4.18.C.4 ESD Training** - All employees with functions that involve any handling, storage, packaging, preservation, or delivery of ESD-sensitive products shall receive training in electrostatic discharge (ESD) protection prior to performing their jobs.

**4.18.C.5  Advanced Quality Training** - The supplier shall offer training in statistical techniques, process capability, statistical sampling, data collection and analysis, problem identification, problem analysis, and corrective and preventive action, as appropriate. [5]

**4.18.C.6  Training Content** – Where hazardous conditions exist, training content should include the following:
a)  Task execution;
b)  Personal safety;
c)  Awareness of hazardous environment; and
d)  Equipment protection.

## Servicing - Element 4.19

> *Where servicing is a specified requirement, the supplier shall establish and maintain documented procedures for performing, verifying and reporting that the servicing meets the specified requirements.*

**4.19.C.1 Supplier's Support Program** - The supplier's quality program shall ensure that customers are provided support to resolve product related problems. [5]

**4.19.C.2 Service Resources** - The supplier shall provide customer contact employees with appropriate tools, training, and resources necessary to provide effective and timely customer service. [4]

**4.19.C.3 Notification About Problems** - The supplier shall establish and maintain a documented procedure(s) to notify all customers who may be affected by a reported problem that is service affecting. [5]

**4.19.C.4 Problem Severity** - The customer and supplier shall jointly assign severity levels to customer reported problems based on the impact to the customer. The severity level shall be used in determining the timeliness of the supplier's response. [10]

**4.19.C.5 Problem Escalation** - The supplier shall establish and maintain documented escalation procedure(s) to resolve customer reported problems. [10]

**4.19.H.1 Supplier's Recall Process** - The supplier shall establish and maintain a documented procedure(s) for identifying and recalling products that are unfit to remain in service.

**4.19.HS.1 Emergency Service** - The supplier shall ensure that services and resources are available to support recovery from emergency failures of product in the field throughout its expected life. [4]

**4.19.HS.2 Problem Resolution Configuration Management** - The supplier shall establish an interface between problem resolution and configuration management to ensure that fixes to problems are incorporated in future revisions. [10]

**4.19.HS.3 Installation Plan** - The supplier shall establish and maintain a documented installation plan. The installation plan shall identify resources, information, and installation events. Installation events and results shall be documented. [9]

**4.19.S.1 Patching Procedure(s)** - The supplier shall establish and maintain documented procedure(s) that guide the decision to solve problems by patching.
a)   This documented procedure(s) shall address patch development procedures, propagation (forward and backward), and resolution.
b)   This documented procedure(s) shall be consistent with purchaser needs or contractual requirements for maintenance support.
c)   For each patch, the supplier shall provide the customer with a statement of impact regarding that patch on the customer's operation. [10]

**4.19.S.2  Problem Resolution** - The supplier shall establish and maintain documented procedure(s) to initiate corrective action once a reported trouble is diagnosed as a problem.  The documented procedure(s) should provide guidelines for distinguishing among potential solutions such as:
a)   Patching;
b)   Immediate source code corrections;
c)   Deferring solutions to a planned release; and
d)   Providing documented "work-around" operational procedure(s) and resolution within a designated timeframe based on the severity of the issue. [10]

## Statistical Techniques - Element 4.20

| | |
|---|---|
| **Identification of Need 4.20.1** | *The supplier shall identify the need for statistical techniques required for establishing, controlling, and verifying process capability and product characteristics.* |

**4.20.1.C.1 Process Measurement** - Process measurements shall be developed, documented, and monitored at appropriate points to ensure continued suitability and promote increased effectiveness of processes. [8]

| | |
|---|---|
| **Procedures 4.20.2** | *The supplier shall establish and maintain documented procedures to implement and control the application of the statistical techniques identified in 4.20.1.* |

## Quality Improvement and Customer Satisfaction - Element 4.21

**Quality Improvement Program 4.21.1**

**4.21.1.C.1 Quality Improvement Program** - The supplier shall establish and maintain a documented Quality Improvement Program to improve:
a) Customer satisfaction;
b) Quality and reliability of the product; and
c) Other processes/product/services used within the company. [5]

**C-NOTE V:** Inputs to the continuous improvement process may include lessons learned from past experience, lessons learned from previous projects, analysis of metrics and post-project reviews, and comparisons with industry best practices.

**4.21.1.C.2 Employee Participation** - The supplier shall have methods for encouraging employee participation in the quality improvement process. [4]

**4.21.1.C.3 Supplier Performance Feedback** - The supplier shall inform employees of its quality performance and the level of customer satisfaction. [4]

**Customer-Supplier Relationship 4.21.2**

**4.21.2.C.1 Management Commitment** - Management with executive responsibility shall demonstrate active involvement in establishing and maintaining customer-supplier relationships. [4]

**4.21.2.C.2 Customer-Supplier Communication** - The supplier shall establish and maintain a documented procedure(s), for communicating with selected customers. The documented procedure(s) shall include:
a) A strategy and criteria for customer selection;
b) A method for sharing customer and supplier expectations and improving the quality of products; and
c) A joint review with the customer at defined intervals covering the status of customer-supplier shared expectations and including a method to track the resolution of issues. [4]

**C-NOTE W:** It is recognized that it is not possible for a supplier to provide the same level of communication with all its customers. The level provided may depend upon the amount of business with the customer, the history of problems, customer expectations, and other factors. See the Appendix, "Guidance for Customer-Supplier Communication."

**Quality Results 4.21.3**

**4.21.3.C.1 Customer Satisfaction** - The supplier shall establish and maintain a method to collect data directly from customers concerning their satisfaction with provided products. The supplier shall also collect customer data on how well the supplier meets commitments and its responsiveness to customer feedback and needs. This data shall be collected and analyzed, and trends shall be kept. [4]

**4.21.3.H.1 Field Performance Data** - The quality system shall include the collection and analysis of field performance data which can be used to help identify the cause and frequency of equipment failure. In addition, no trouble found (NTF) data shall also be maintained. This information shall be provided to the appropriate organizations to foster continuous improvement. The quality system shall include a documented procedure(s) to provide the customer with feedback on their complaints in a timely manner. [5]

**4.21.3.V.1 Service Performance Data** –The quality system shall include the collection and analysis of service performance data, which can be used to identify the cause and frequency of service failures. This information shall be provided to the appropriate organizations to foster continuous improvement of the service. [5]

---

**New Product Introduction 4.21.4**

**4.21.4.C.1 New Product Introduction** - The supplier shall establish and maintain documented procedure(s) for introducing new products.

**C-NOTE X:** The new product introduction program should include provisions for such programs as: quality and reliability prediction studies, pilot production, demand and capacity studies, sales and service personnel training, and new product post-introduction evaluations.

# Appendix A: TL 9000 Accreditation Body Implementation Requirements

Below are requirements with regard to TL 9000 implementation including criteria for registrar qualification, registrar auditor qualifications, certificates, and upgrading of registrar accreditation to include TL 9000. These requirements will apply to all QuEST Forum-recognized accreditation bodies and the registrars qualified by these accreditation bodies to conduct TL 9000 registrations.

## 1. Accredited Registrars

Accredited registrars shall:

1.1 Provide accreditation bodies with written agreement to conduct TL 9000 registrations in compliance with "Code of Practice for TL 9000 Registrars."

1.2 Provide accreditation bodies, prior to beginning TL 9000 registrations, relevant documentation showing that the registrar process complies with the "Code of Practice for TL 9000 Registrars," and the registrar requirements in this appendix.

1.3 Maintain a listing of their TL 9000 qualified auditors.

1.4 Have personnel on the governing board/council of experts that have telecommunications industry experience, as well as expertise in the appropriate NAICS/SIC (North American Industry Classification System) or NACE codes for their scope, as defined by the current accreditation body practice.

1.5 Have at least one member of the registration decision making body who has successfully completed and passed the exam of the sector-specific training referred to in 1.10 b). This member shall have veto power with regard to TL 9000 registration decisions.

1.6 Utilize an audit team, which has at least one (1) member with relevant experience in the telecommunications industry. Refer to the QuEST Forum Web page "Registrar Information".

1.7 Not use the TL 9000 notation on certificates until after the accreditation body has witnessed and approved a registrar's TL 9000 audit.

1.8 Be permitted, after the witness audit has been satisfactorily completed, to update the ISO 9001 certificates to TL 9000 certificates of previously assessed companies who were found to be in compliance with TL 9000. The registrar shall obtain a witness audit within three (3) months or six (6) audits of their initial TL 9000 audit and shall be subject to 2.1 below. Where the registrar does not satisfactorily complete the witness audit, the registrar shall be responsible for remedies for any previously assessed companies appropriate to the content and severity of the problems discovered, and as agreed upon by the accreditation body. No additional TL 9000 audits shall be permitted until the registrar's corrective actions are accepted by the accreditation body.

1.9 Be permitted to use a full TL 9000 or an ISO 9001 upgrade to TL 9000 as a witness assessment.

1.10 Utilize auditors that:
    a) Are recognized and qualified as ISO 9001 auditors per the accreditation body's criteria;
    b) Are sector-specific qualified by the QuEST Forum as evidenced by a certificate sent to the registrar (upon successful completion of a Forum certified training program);
    c) Have relevant experience in the activity being audited.

1.11 Provide certificates of registration to TL 9000 compliant organizations citing conformance to TL 9000 and the relevant ISO 9001:1994 standard.

1.12 Define delisting criteria, and steps for delisting registrants.

1.13 Be responsible for remedies for any TL 9000 registrants affected by the delisting of the registrar by the accreditation body, appropriate to the severity of the problems discovered. The accreditation body shall agree upon these remedies.

1.14 Provide transition support for future TL 9000 releases consistent with the Forum's guidance and transition plan.

## 2. Accreditation Bodies

Accreditation bodies shall:

2.1 Be responsible for providing an auditor (audit team) to witness one (1) of the initial six (6) TL 9000 audits of any ISO 9001 accredited registrar completing items 1.1 and 1.2 above (see 1.8). The accreditation body shall notify the Forum Administrator of the date when each registrar has successfully completed the witnessing above.

2.2 Be responsible in the conduct of witnessing for utilizing any outside experts or observers needed. This responsibility shall include avoidance of conflict of interest, availability, and timeliness.

2.3 Define:
a) Delisting criteria, and steps for delisting TL 9000 qualified registrars, and
b) An appropriate process for appeal of a witnessing decision or any other steps in the TL 9000 process.

2.4 Maintain a "TL 9000 Qualified Registrar Listing" kept up-to-date and distributed to the Forum Administrator whenever the listing changes. These lists shall note new additions or deletions from previous revisions. Notice of loss of accreditation shall be formally communicated promptly to the Forum Administrator.

2.5 Provide a certificate, or similar formal notification, that can be used to document the registrar's qualification, to each qualified TL 9000 registrar who has met all requirements of TL 9000. Refer to the Appendix, "Code of Practice for TL 9000 Registrars," and this document.

2.6 Provide transition support for future TL 9000 releases consistent with the Forum's guidance and transition plan.

## 3. The QuEST Forum

The QuEST Forum shall:

3.1 Establish the Forum Administrator as the central point of contact to act as the clearinghouse for all inquiries, accreditation, registrar and certification related items, issues, and concerns.

3.2 Share appropriate TL 9000 communications with their recognized accreditation bodies.

3.3 Recognize any accreditation body that is a signatory to the IAF (International Accreditation Forum) MLA (Multi Lateral Agreement). The Forum will recognize the witness audits of such registrars for the TL 9000 launch. These accreditation bodies are encouraged to implement a mutual recognition of each other's witness audits, described herein above, in support of the TL 9000 launch.

3.4 Provide guidance and a transition plan for the introduction of future TL 9000 releases.

# Appendix B: Code of Practice for TL 9000 Registrars

The registrars must be accredited by a body recognized by the QuEST Forum. The registrar's scope of accreditation shall cover the activity being registered (i.e., Hardware, Software, or Services, or any combination).

The assessment shall include evaluation of all company quality system elements for effective implementation of TL 9000 requirements. Part of the evidence shall include the results of at least one complete internal audit cycle and management review.

It is permissible for each surveillance audit to re-examine part of the system so that the equivalent of a total reassessment is completed within each three-year cycle. The Audit Report shall clearly show the part of the system that was audited on each surveillance visit.

The audit team shall provide a full report on the operation audited per Model B of the current RvA publication, *Guideline for Compiling Reports on Quality System Audits*, to the company within forty-five (45) days of each initial and surveillance (partial) audit unless otherwise agreed by the company. Third-party auditors will identify nonconformances and opportunities for improvement, as these become evident during the audit, without recommending specific solutions. These nonconformances and opportunities shall be included in the report to the company.

Registrars, or bodies related to a registrar, that have provided quality system consulting services and/or private training to a particular client may not conduct registration services for that client, nor may they supply auditors.

Each member of the registrar's team performing audits to TL 9000 requirements shall have satisfactorily completed TL 9000 courses that have been approved by the QuEST Forum. Also, a majority of those responsible for making certification decisions, or at least one with veto, shall satisfactorily complete this training. A certificate will indicate satisfactory completion.

Quality system consultants to the company, if present during the assessment, are limited to the role of observer.

All structural or systemic (e.g., Major) nonconformances which could affect product quality shall be resolved prior to the issuance of the TL 9000 Certificate. All nonconformances are handled in accordance with the registrar's standard operating procedure(s).

Registrars are authorized to cite conformance to TL 9000 on ISO certificates, when they:
a) Contract with a supplier to follow this Code of Practice; and
b) Are accredited by a QuEST Forum-recognized accreditation body to issue TL 9000 certificates.

The registrar must have a process to settle disputes over interpretations of the standard.

# Appendix C:  Registration Procedures

**Registration procedures**

The following steps are suggested as a procedure for a company that has decided to obtain TL 9000 registration.

a) Determine the scope of the registration.

b) If not already in place, develop and implement (changes to) a documented quality management system so that it meets or exceeds the TL 9000 requirements.

c) Conduct a self-assessment and implement any needed improvements to comply with the TL 9000 requirements.

d) Contract with a TL 9000 accredited registrar to conduct the registration in accordance with the selected scope.

e) Follow the registrar's process of registration and surveillance audits to obtain and maintain the TL 9000 certificate (see the Appendix, "Alternate Method for Maintaining TL 9000 Certification/Registration").

# Appendix D: Migration Path and Audit Days

This section applies only to Hardware, Software and Services Quality System Requirements.

The Forum recognizes the achievement of existing quality systems efforts. These efforts will be leveraged in the migration path to TL 9000. To follow any of the migration paths below, the TL 9000 candidate must have a current registration to a recognized Quality System Registration. The scope of the existing registration shall be compared to the scope of the TL 9000 registration being sought; any addition to the existing scope must be assessed to the complete TL 9000.

The following Quality System Registrations are currently recognized:
a) ISO 9001
b) ISO 9002
c) CSQP$^{SM}$
d) QS-9000

Other Quality Systems will be recognized as necessary, for example:
a) SEI CMM
b) TickIT

This migration process is only to be used during the initial registration process; all subsequent assessment activities will be conducted per standard registration procedures.

**Migration Paths**

The migration paths listed below assume that the TL 9000 candidate is currently registered to the quality system listed. All areas not included in the scope of the original registration shall be subjected to TL 9000 in its entirety. See the Requirements Origin Table in this appendix for details.

**ISO 9001 to TL 9000**
The TL 9000 sections associated with the following industry standards will not need to be assessed during the **initial audit**:
• ISO 9001 - all italicized requirements

ISO 9002 to TL 9000
The TL 9000 sections associated with the following industry standards will not need to be assessed during the **initial audit**:
• ISO 9001 - all italicized requirements except those within the Design Control Element 4.4 which may need to be assessed depending on the stated scope of the supplier's registration.

**CSQP$^{sm}$ & ISO 9001 to TL 9000**
The TL 9000 sections associated with the following industry standards will not need to be assessed during the **initial audit**:
• GR-1202-CORE – all requirements followed by the endnote, [4]
• TR-NWT-000179 - all requirements followed by the endnote, [10]
• GR-1252-CORE - all requirements followed by the endnote, [5]
• ISO 9001 - all italicized requirements

**QS-9000 & ISO 9001 to TL 9000**

The TL 9000 sections associated with the following industry standards will not need to be assessed during the **initial audit:**

- Customer Satisfaction – all requirements under 4.21
- ISO 9001- all italicized requirements

---

**Audit Days Table**

The Audit Days Table defines the **minimum** number of audit-days needed to achieve and maintain TL 9000 registration. Various schemes are described along with recommended industry compliance time frames.

The table shows the **minimum** number of on-site audit days that should be spent by the registrar on the initial TL 9000/ISO 9001 quality system audits and ongoing surveillance audits.

Registrars will document actual audit days. Any deviation greater than 0.5 on-site auditor days under the **minimum** on-site audit days total is to be documented and submitted to the Registrar's Accreditation Body within five (5) working days after the quotation date. No certificate for TL 9000 is to be issued until the submitted deviation has been concurred in writing by the accreditation body. The audit can proceed but the Registrar shall advise the Supplier of the risk involved if the accreditation body requires additional audit days.

The Accreditation Body shall respond within ten (10) working days of receipt of the Registrar's written request for reducing the **minimum** on-site audit days. The accreditation body will confirm its written agreement or rejection.

Use of this table by registrars is effective immediately and remains in effect until modified by the QuEST Forum. The most current version of the Audit Days Table is available on the QuEST Forum Web page (www.questforum.org) or from the QuEST Forum Administrator.

**Requirements Origin**

The table below depicts the original source for each TL 9000 requirement. Requirements that are being introduced with the TL 9000 Handbook will be associated with the label "QuEST Forum" in the source document column. Please note that only the ISO 9001 requirements are consistently reproduced verbatim. All other requirements have been modified. (See Table 2)

| TL 9000 Requirement | Source Document | | | | | | | |
|---|---|---|---|---|---|---|---|---|
| | ISO 9001 | GR-1202 | GR-1252 | TR-179 | ISO 12207 | QuEST Forum | ISO 9000-3 | ISO 9004-2 |
| 4.1.1 | X | | | | | | | |
| 4.1.1.C.1 | | | | | | X | | |
| 4.1.2 | X | | | | | | | |
| 4.1.2.1 | X | | | | | | | |
| 4.1.2.2 | X | | | | | | | |
| 4.1.2.3 | X | | | | | | | |
| 4.1.3 | X | | | | | | | |
| 4.2.1 | X | | | | | | | |
| 4.2.2 | X | | | | | | | |
| 4.2.2.C.1 | | | | | 5.2.4.2 | | | |
| 4.2.2.S.1 | | | | (R)-4.6-7 | | | | |
| 4.2.3 | X | | | | | | | |
| 4.2.3.C.1 | | R2-18 | | | | | | |
| 4.2.3.C.2 | | R2-19 | | | | | | |
| 4.2.3.C.3 | | R2-20 | | | | | | |
| 4.2.3.C.4 | | | | | 6.2.6.1 | | | |
| 4.3.1 | X | | | | | | | |
| 4.3.2 | X | | | | | | | |
| C-NOTE B | | | | | | | 4.3.2 | |
| C-NOTE C | | | | | 5.1.5.1 | | | |
| 4.3.3 | X | | | | | | | |
| 4.3.4 | X | | | | | | | |
| 4.4.1 | X | | | | | | | |
| 4.4.1.C.1 | | | | 4.1.3-4 | | | | |
| 4.4.2 | X | | | | | | | |
| 4.4.2.C.1 | | | | | 5.2.4.5 | | | |
| 4.4.2.C.2 | | | | 3.7.1 | | | | |
| 4.4.2.C.3 | | | | | 5.5.6.1 | | | |
| 4.4.2.S.1 | | | | (R) 3.4.3-1 | | | | |
| 4.4.2.S.2 | | | | (R) 3.4.3-3 | | | | |
| 4.4.2.S.3 | | | | | 5.3.8.1 | | | |
| 4.4.2.S.4 | | | | | 5.5.5.2-3 | | | |
| 4.4.3 | X | | | | | | | |
| 4.4.4 | X | | | | | | | |
| 4.4.4.C.1 | | R2-10 | | | | | | |
| 4.4.4.C.2 | | | | | 5.3.2.1-2 | | | |
| 4.4.4.H.1 | | | R2-12 | | | | | |

| TL 9000 Requirement | Source Document | | | | | | | |
|---|---|---|---|---|---|---|---|---|
| | ISO 9001 | GR-1202 | GR-1252 | TR-179 | ISO 12207 | QuEST Forum | ISO 9000-3 | ISO 9004-2 |
| 4.4.4.S.1 | | | | | 5.3.4.1 | | | |
| 4.4.4.S.2 | | | | | | | 4.4.4.c | |
| 4.4.5 | X | | | | | | | |
| 4.4.5.S.1 | | | | | | | 4.4.5 | |
| 4.4.5.V.1 | | | | | | | | 6.2.3 |
| 4.4.6 | X | | | | | | | |
| 4.4.7 | X | | | | | | | |
| 4.4.8 | X | | | | | | | |
| 4.4.8.H.1 | | | R2-13 | | | | | |
| 4.4.8.H.2 | | | R2-14 | | | | | |
| 4.4.8.H.3 | | | R2-15 | | | | | |
| 4.4.9 | X | | | | | | | |
| 4.4.9.C.1 | | | R2-8 | | | | | |
| 4.4.9.C.2 | | | R2-11 | | | | | |
| 4.4.9.H.1 | | | R2-16 | | | | | |
| 4.4.9.H.2 | | | | | | X | | |
| 4.4.9.V.1 | | | | | | X | | |
| 4.5.1 | X | | | | | | | |
| 4.5.1.S.1 | | | | | | X | | |
| 4.5.2 | X | | | | | | | |
| 4.5.3 | X | | | | | | | |
| 4.6.1 | X | | | | | | | |
| 4.6.1.C.1 | | | R2-20 | | 5.1.1.8; 5.1.3.1 | | | |
| 4.6.2 | X | | | | | | | |
| 4.6.3 | X | | | | | | | |
| 4.6.4 | X | | | | | | | |
| 4.6.4.1 | X | | | | | | | |
| 4.6.4.2 | X | | | | | | | |
| 4.7 | X | | | | | | | |
| 4.8 | X | | | | | | | |
| 4.8.H.1 | | | | | | X | | |
| 4.8.H.2 | | | | | | X | | |
| 4.8.HS.1 | | | | | 6.2.1.1 – 6.2.2.1 | | | |
| 4.8.HS.2 | | | | | | | 4.8 | |
| 4.9 | X | | | | | | | |
| 4.9.H.1 | | | R2-25 | | | | | |
| 4.9.HV.1 | | | R2-26 | | | | | |
| 4.9.HV.2 | | R2-37 | | | | | | |
| 4.9.HV.3 | | R2-38 | | | | | | |
| 4.9.S.1 | | | | | | | 4.9 | |
| 4.9.S.2 | | | | (R) 3.9.1-2,3 | 5.5.5.3, 5.5.6.2, 6.2.6.1 | | | |
| 4.9.V.1 | | | | | | X | | |

| TL 9000 Requirement | Source Document | | | | | | | |
|---|---|---|---|---|---|---|---|---|
| | ISO 9001 | GR-1202 | GR-1252 | TR-179 | ISO 12207 | QuEST Forum | ISO 9000-3 | ISO 9004-2 |
| 4.9.V.2 | | | | | 5.2.4.5 | | | |
| 4.10.1 | X | | | | | | | |
| 4.10.1.HV.1 | | | R2-5 | | | | | |
| 4.10.1.S.1 | | | | 3.7.1,2 | | | | |
| 4.10.2 | X | | | | | | | |
| 4.10.2.1 | X | | | | | | | |
| 4.10.2.2 | X | | | | | | | |
| 4.10.2.3 | X | | | | | | | |
| 4.10.3 | X | | | | | | | |
| 4.10.4 | X | | | | | | | |
| 4.10.4.H.1 | | | R2-28 | | | | | |
| 4.10.4.H.2 | | | | | | X | | |
| 4.10.5 | X | | | | | | | |
| 4.10.5.HV.1 | | | R2-42 | | | | | |
| 4.11.1 | X | | | | | | | |
| 4.11.2 | X | | | | | | | |
| 4.11.2.H.1 | | | R2-31 | | | | | |
| 4.12 | X | | | | | | | |
| 4.13.1 | X | | | | | | | |
| 4.13.2 | X | | | | | | | |
| 4.13.2.C.1 | | | | | | X | | |
| 4.14.1 | X | | | | | | | |
| 4.14.2 | X | | | | | | | |
| 4.14.3 | X | | | | | | | |
| 4.15.1 | X | | | | | | | |
| 4.15.1.C.1 | | | R2-38 | | | | | |
| 4.15.1.C.2 | | | R2-39 | | | | | |
| 4.15.2 | X | | | | | | | |
| 4.15.2.S.1 | | | | | | | 4.15.2; 4.15.6 | |
| 4.15.3 | X | | | | | | | |
| 4.15.3.H.1 | | | R2-40 | | | | | |
| 4.15.4 | X | | | | | | | |
| 4.15.5 | X | | | | | | | |
| 4.15.6 | X | | | | | | | |
| 4.15.6.S.1 | | | | 3.9.4-2 | | | | |
| 4.16 | X | | | | | | | |
| 4.17 | X | | | | | | | |
| 4.18 | X | | | | | | | |
| 4.18.C.1 | | R2-36 | | | | | | |
| 4.18.C.2 | | R2-34 | | | | | | |
| 4.18.C.3 | | R2-32,35 | | | | | | |
| 4.18.C.4 | | | | | | X | | |
| 4.18.C.5 | | | R2-56 | | | | | |
| 4.18.C.6 | | | | | | X | | |

| TL 9000 Requirement | Source Document | | | | | | | |
|---|---|---|---|---|---|---|---|---|
| | ISO 9001 | GR-1202 | GR-1252 | TR-179 | ISO 12207 | QuEST Forum | ISO 9000-3 | ISO 9004-2 |
| 4.19 | X | | | | | | | |
| 4.19.C.1 | | | R2-52 | | | | | |
| 4.19.C.2 | | R2-16 | | | | | | |
| 4.19.C.3 | | | R2-54 | | | | | |
| 4.19.C.4 | | | | 4.10.2-7,8 | | | | |
| 4.19.C.5 | | | | 4.10.2-6 | | | | |
| 4.19.H.1 | | | | | | X | | |
| 4.19.HS.1 | | R2-17 | | | | | | |
| 4.19.HS.2 | | | | 4.10.2-9 | | | | |
| 4.19.HS.3 | | | | | 5.3.12, 5.3.12.2, 5.5.5.4-5, 5.5.6.3-5 | | | |
| 4.19.S.1 | | | | 3.10.3-1 | | | | |
| 4.19.S.2 | | | | 4.10.2.5 | | | | |
| 4.20.1 | X | | | | | | | |
| 4.20.1.C.1 | | | | | | | 4.20 | |
| 4.20.2 | X | | | | | | | |
| 4.21.1.C.1 | | | R2-57 | | | | | |
| 4.21.1.C.2 | | R2-26 | | | | | | |
| 4.21.1.C.3 | | R2-31 | | | | | | |
| 4.21.2.C.1 | | R2-7 | | | | | | |
| 4.21.2.C.2 | | R2-9,15,18 | | | | | | |
| 4.21.3.C.1 | | R2-46 | | | | | | |
| 4.21.3.H.1 | | | R2-46 | | | | | |
| 4.21.3.V.1 | | | R2-46 | | | | | |
| 4.21.4.C.1 | | | | | | X | | |
| | | | | | | | | |

Table 2: Source Documents

TL 9000 Quality System Requirements

# Appendix E: Alternative Method for Maintaining TL 9000 Certification/Registration

(From the International Accreditation Forum, Working Group III, January 21, 1998)

## 1. Objectives and Principles

The "Alternative Method for Maintaining TL 9000 Certification/Registration" (AM) is a method to determine if a supplier's quality management system meets the ISO 9001 criteria to warrant continuation of an accredited certification by a third party (I) (See Figure 2). The method is based on utilizing the supplier's (first party) internal audit system as a complement to the certifier's/registrar's (third party) own assessment activities.

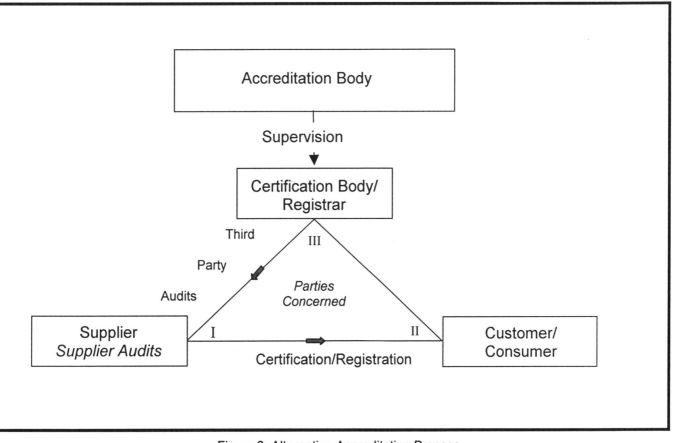

Figure 2: Alternative Accreditation Process

The objectives are elimination of unnecessary audit duplication and improving the effectiveness of third party TL 9000 audits and certification/registration. Higher value can be achieved by increasing benefits or decreasing costs to "customers." However, the primary goal is not to decrease costs but is to add value when compared to other more traditional methods of third party auditing.  The aim is more added value compared to other methods of "third-party" auditing (II).

Advantages to the supplier are (III):
Recognition of a common and consistently implemented quality system;
Reduced costs of maintaining certification/registration as a result of:
— Reduced on-site days of certifiers/registrars;
— Site sampling which reduces plant interruptions; and
— Enhanced monitoring of internal audits by certifiers/registrars.
More robust internal audit system;
Improved communication among certifiers/registrars and suppliers.

Advantages to "third parties" are:
- Improving effectiveness of "third-party auditing"; and
- In depth auditing possible by monitoring internal audits.

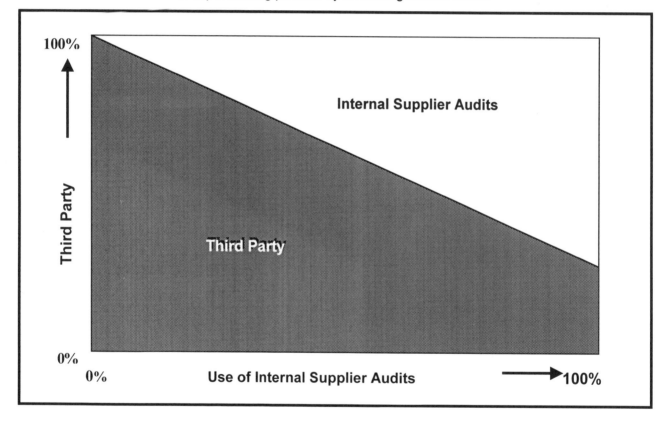

Figure 3:  Internal Supplier Audits

The extent to which internal audit results are taken into account depends on a number of factors such as the structure of the quality organization, the maturity of the quality system, and the possibility for verification by the certification body/registrar. When appropriate, existing guidelines for sampling may apply in external audits.

The AM approach is applicable only if a number of requirements (qualification/eligibility criteria) have been met by the supplier and can be verified by the certification body/registrar. The AM approach is in general:

- Available to any supplier who meets the qualification criteria, without any discrimination with respect to size of sites, number of sites or sector of industry.
- Restricted to third-party surveillance and re-assessment audits.
- Applicable only if:

  a) The supplier's quality system fully complies with all TL 9000 requirements as determined by an accredited third-party registrar;
  b) The supplier's internal audit system is effective and its results reflect accurately the actual status of the quality system and its compliance with TL 9000;
  c) The supplier is capable of demonstrating with its management review that the management is in full control and command of goals/objectives and routinely takes adequate preventive and corrective actions.
  Never restricted only to supplier's internal audits, independent "third-party" auditing will always remain to maintain the impartiality and effectiveness of the certification/registration process.

## 2. Qualification/ Eligibility Criteria for Suppliers

- The supplier must have a quality management system in conformance with TL 9000, for a period of at least three years. Accredited certification/registration meets the intent of this requirement.
- The supplier shall demonstrate customer satisfaction within its industry of operation, by:
  — Customer satisfaction responses; and
  — Acceptable delivered quality, warranty/customer returns and delivery.
- The supplier can demonstrate to have a centrally coordinated system for:
  — Internal auditing which adheres to ISO 10011; and
  — Corrective and preventive actions based on audit results and customers complaints.
- The supplier's management shall demonstrate its commitment to quality and improvements of quality objectives and results in a quantified way over a period of time exceeding two years.
- Each internal auditor should have a sufficient background in the activities he has to evaluate and a good knowledge of the applicable procedures but should be independent from the persons having a direct responsibility in the performance of those activities (e.g., he may work for another department or unit).

## 3. Qualification Assessment by Certification Body/Registrar

As a first step in the application of the AM approach the accredited certification body/registrar will carry out a qualification assessment, in which the qualification criteria are verified.

The certification body/registrar reserves the right to select the audit sites and TL 9000 elements to be sampled.

In the verification of the criteria the certification body/registrar looks for evidence of effectiveness of the supplier's quality performance over the last three (3) years. This evidence shall be gathered based on earlier surveillance audit results, results from independent customer satisfaction surveys and customer complaints.

The certification body/registrar shall have access to results of all phases of the management control process for quality, including results of management reviews and corrective and preventive actions. The auditing results will be reviewed by the certification body/registrar.

In addition the certification body/registrar investigates and verifies the effectiveness of the supplier's internal audit system and the compliance with the relevant criteria, namely:

The supplier must have an effective internal audit system in which audit teams are independent from the unit/activity to be audited, to avoid conflicts of interest.

— Internal audits shall regularly cover all requirements of TL 9000.
— Internal audits shall be scheduled on the basis of the status and importance of the activities.
— Internal audits shall be carried out in accordance with ISO 10011.
— Internal lead auditors shall be qualified in accordance with ISO 10011 by an external independent organization.

## 4. Qualification/ Eligibility Criteria for Certification Bodies/Registrars

In order to utilize the AM approach the certification body/registrar must be able to design an approach that meets the unique requirements of the suppliers quality system. The design process of the certification body/registrar must operate in full conformance to TL 9000. The accreditation body may verify the design capability of the certification body/registrar.

- In principle the qualification criteria for certification bodies/registrars who want to apply the AM approach can be derived from qualification criteria for the suppliers:
  — The certification body/registrar has been accredited in accordance with ISO/IEC Guide 62 (EN 45012) requirements for at least three (3) years.
  — The certification body/registrar can demonstrate improvement of service quality objectives and results over a period of three (3) years.

**. Limitations**

- In any phase of the qualification for or the implementation of the AM program that the certification body/registrar finds evidence that any requirements are not satisfied (or not any more), the AM program shall be suspended. The certification body/registrar shall then apply its normal procedures with full audit coverage of all sites and activities of the supplier. This option, on the part of the registrar, is to be incorporated in a contractual agreement.

- When appropriate, existing IAF guidelines (e.g., for sampling rates) will be applied in the AM audit program of the certification body/registrar. The design of the AM audit program will be different for each case, because it must be tailored to the specific circumstances.

# Appendix F: Guidance for Customer-Supplier Communications

Below are four (4) sample approaches that may be used in customer-supplier communications. Other approaches may be applicable to your business situation.

### Approach A: Shared Expectations Team

One approach to customer-supplier communications is a voluntary shared expectations process. This is a process in which a single supplier works jointly with a customer to create an understanding of each other's expectations and improve quality on a continuing basis. The objective is a closer, long-term relationship between the two participants.

A joint team of supplier and customer personnel is formed to review expectations, identify gaps and create the mechanism for reducing the gaps. An impartial, telecommunications-experienced facilitator may be added to the team when agreed to by both customer and supplier. The team develops action items and tracks them on an action item register. Often, action items are worked on by joint customer-supplier task forces. Costs are shared by the customer and supplier.

It is recommended that the team will meet at least twice a year. A number of tools are used for continual quality improvement, including the action item register and quality improvement methodologies. A typical agenda for the initial meeting is as follows:
a) Customer expectations;
b) Supplier expectations;
c) Compare current performance against expectations;
d) Identify gaps;
e) Develop action plans to address the gaps; and
f) Define measures to track and monitor the action plans.

### Approach B: Quality Review Meetings

To facilitate communications, customers and suppliers are encouraged to have periodic meetings to discuss the supplier's quality system. It is recommended that meetings alternate between the supplier location and customer site where equipment furnished by the supplier is in operation.

Sample meeting agenda for supplier location meeting:
a) Any nonconformances to TL 9000;
b) Sample of internal audit reports and related improvement actions;
c) Metrics;
d) Engineering complaints;
e) Product change notices;
f) Customer concerns;
g) Supplier concerns; and
h) Action item register (AIR).

### Customer Site Visit

Meet at customer site where supplier's equipment has been operating for less than one year (preferably 3 to 6 months). All customer functions that were directly involved with the engineering, procurement, turn-up, and operation of the equipment are invited to participate along with the supplier representatives, which may include the program and/or product managers, quality and sales representatives, and others as appropriate.

The purpose of the visit is to obtain feedback on the entire process of procuring and operating equipment plus related services. Based on customer participants, the feedback would address some or all of the following:
a) Quality and reliability of hardware and software;
b) Ease of ordering;
c) Supplier representatives;
d) New product introduction;
e) Product delivery;
f) Technical support;
g) Documentation;
h) Product Change Notices (PCNs);
i) Invoices;
j) Installation;
k) Repair; and
l) Training.

Other customer or supplier concerns should be discussed as well as a review/update to the action item register.

The feedback obtained in this visit should be documented and any issues included in an action item register with planned improvement actions by supplier and/or customer.

### Approach C: Customized Reports

Supplier provides periodic reports based on customer identified needs. Such reports may include:
a)   Hardware return rates;
b)   Delivery performance;
c)   Repair turnaround time;
d)   Reported problems;
e)   Technical support activity; and
f)   Other.

**Approach D: Program Reviews**
Conduct periodic program reviews at customer or supplier location with an agenda that may include:
a)   Current deliveries;
b)   Forecast of future requirements;
c)   Technical issues;
d)   Product feature requests/needs;
e)   Quality issues;
f)   Ordering/invoicing issues;
g)   Improvement opportunities relative to supplier products; and
h)   Customer-supplier interface.

The action item register should be maintained and action items reported on at each review or more often, if appropriate.

# Glossary

**Accredited Registrars**

Accredited Registrars are qualified organizations certified by a national body (e.g., the Registrar Accreditation Board in the U.S.) to perform audits to the TL 9000 and to register the auditee when they are shown to be compliant to the TL 9000 requirements.

**Anti-Static Protection**

A method or procedure(s) used to dissipate completely or almost completely the static charge from a source before it can reach devices, or products that are sensitive to electrostatic discharge. The source could be a human body, clothing, or other partially conducting materials and insulators.

**Audit**

A planned independent and documented assessment to determine whether agreed-upon requirements are being met. See also, *quality audit*.

**Backward Traceability**

Ability to trace the history, application, or location of an item or activity and like items or activities by means of recorded identification back to the source.

**Certification**

Procedure(s) by which a third party gives written assurance that a product \, process or quality management system conforms to specified requirements.

**Certification Mark**

The mark used to indicate successful assessment to and compliance with the requirements of a quality management system.

**Compliance**

An affirmative indication or judgment that a product has met the requirements of the relevant specifications, contract or regulation; also the state of meeting the requirements.

**Concession**

The authorization to use or release a product which does not conform to specified requirements.

**Configuration Management**

A discipline applying technical and administrative direction and surveillance to: identify and document the functional and physical characteristics of a configuration item, control changes to those characteristics, record and report changes processing and implementation status, and verify compliance with specified requirements.

**Conformance**

An affirmative indication or judgment that a product, process or system has met the requirements of the relevant specification, contract, or regulation.

**Corrective Action**

Action taken to eliminate the causes of an existing nonconformity, defect, or other undesirable situation in order to prevent recurrence.

**Cost of Poor Quality**

The overall financial loss to the business due to problems; the cost of poor quality

**(COPQ)**  includes all costs of rework, lost value, and other forms of wastes that might be prevented through quality methods.  Internal and external costs associated with producing or delivering an imperfect product.

**Critical Problem**  A classification of problem reports.  Critical problems severely affect service, capacity/traffic, billing, and maintenance capabilities and require immediate corrective action, regardless of time of day or day of the week as viewed by a customer upon discussion with the supplier.  For example:

- A loss of service that is comparable to the total loss of effective functional capability of an entire switching or transport system;
- A reduction in capacity or traffic handling capability such that expected loads cannot be handled; and
- Any loss of safety or emergency capability.

See also *major problem* and *minor problem*.

**Customer**  The recipient of a product provided by a supplier.

**Defect**  The non-fulfillment of intended usage requirements. The departure or absence of one or more quality characteristics from intended usage requirements.

**Design**  (1) The process of defining the architecture, components, interfaces, and other characteristics of a system, component or service. (2) The result of the process in (1).

**Design Change**  Changes affecting form, fit, or function.

**Design Review**  A formal documented comprehensive and systematic examination of a design to evaluate the design requirements and the capability of the design to meet these requirements and identify problems and propose solutions.

**Deviation**  A departure from a plan, specified requirement, or expected result.

**Disaster Recovery**  The ability to respond to an interruption in services by implementing a disaster recovery plan to recover an organization's critical functions.  The disaster recovery plan defines the resources, actions, tasks and data required to recover the business process/function in the event of a disaster.

| | |
|---|---|
| **Discrepancy** | A result of a test, inspection, audit, or review that is other than the most favorable possible result, that is judged worthy of noting in a log. |
| **Effectiveness** | The degree to which a process or activity accomplishes its intended result. |
| **End of Life** | The point in time when a product is declared "Manufacturing Discontinued" and/or product support is limited. |
| **ESD** | Electrostatic discharge. Electrostatic discharge is the transient energy dissipated by devices (such as integrated circuits, printed wiring board assemblies, magnetic tapes and/or disks, and other media used for software or data storage) due to surface resistance from the device and the volume resistance of other materials. Discharge is reduced to harmless levels using mechanical, chemical, and environmental methods to minimize frictional or triboelectric charging. |
| **ESD Training** | Telecommunications electronic components and systems are sensitive to ESD damage and upsets. Handling and grounding techniques, combined with an awareness program designed to enlighten personnel about the hazards of ESD, are the most effective methods for eliminating ESD damage. |
| **Field Replaceable Unit (FRU)** | A distinctly separate part that has been designed so that it may be exchanged at its site of use for the purpose of maintenance or service adjustment. An example of a FRU is a plug-in circuit board. An assembly that is replaced in its entirety when any one of its components fails. In some cases, a field replaceable unit may contain other field replaceable units; for example, a brush and a brush block that can be replaced individually or as a single unit. |
| **Forum** | The Quality Excellence for Suppliers of Telecommunications Leadership Forum ("QuEST Forum"). |
| **Grade** | A category or rank given to entities having the same functional use but different requirements for quality. |

**Information Request (IR)**

An IR is a service request for which a customer with minimal technical expertise and acquaintance with the product could determine or resolve on their own. A request for information (IR) may have one or more of the following characteristics:

- It documents a problem that the customer could have resolved independently of the supplier.
- The customer asks a question on procedures that are covered in the documentation which is shipped with the product.
- The customer asks for information on the supplier's product that will be used to help interface the supplier's product with a competitor's product.
- The customer asks for help on a "problem" that turns out not to be a problem, bug, or failure, but rather is due to a lack of understanding of the product.

**Inspection**

Activities, such as measuring, examining, testing, gauging one or more characteristics of a product and comparing these with specified requirements to determine conformity.

**Integration Planning**

The purpose of integration planning is to ensure that modules within a system release work together as designed and that they interact with external interfaces as designed. Planning is followed by integration testing that is performed to verify that the system works as designed.

**International Accreditation Forum (IAF)**

An international consortium of accreditation bodies.

**International Organization for Standardization**

Also, ISO. A worldwide federation of national standards bodies formed in 1947. ISO produces standards in all fields, except electrical and electronic (which are covered by IEC).

**ISO 9001**

A model for Quality Assurance in design, development, production, installation and servicing.

**Life Cycle Model**

The processes, activities, and tasks involved in the development, operation, and maintenance of products, spanning the life of products.

**Major Problem**

A classification of problem reports. Major problems cause conditions that seriously affect system operation, maintenance, and administration, etc., and require immediate attention as viewed by the customer upon discussion with the supplier. The urgency is less than in critical situations because of a lesser immediate or impending effect on system performance, customers, and the customer's operation and revenue. For example:

- Reduction in any capacity/traffic measurement function;
- Any loss of functional visibility and/or diagnostic capability;
- Short outages equivalent to system or subsystem outages with accumulated duration of greater than two (2) minutes in any twenty-four (24) hour period, or that continue to repeat during longer periods;
- Repeated degradation of DS1 or higher rate spans or connections;
- Prevention of access for routine administrative activity;
- Degradation of access for maintenance or recovery operations;
- Degradation of the system's ability to provide any required Critical or Major Trouble notification;
- Any significant increase in product related customer trouble reports;
- Billing error rates that exceed specifications;
- Corruption of system or billing databases.

See also *critical problem* and *minor problem*.

**Method**

A means by which an activity is accomplished which is not necessarily documented.

**Migration Planning**

When a product is planned to be moved from an old to a new environment, the supplier shall develop and document a migration plan.

**Minor Problem**

A classification of problem reports. Minor problems do not significantly impair the functioning of the system and do not significantly affect service to customers. These problems are tolerable during system use.

See also *critical problem* and *major problem*.

**NACE**

Nomenclature Générale des Activitiés Économique dans les Communautés Européennes.

**Nonconformance**

Non-fulfillment of a requirement.

**Patch**

Any interim software change, such as object code change, or module replacement, to an in-service release.

**Patching Policy**

The overall method of action to guide the development and deployment of an interim software change to an in-service release.

**Plan**

A scheme or method of acting, proceeding, etc. developed in advance.

**Preventive Action**      Action taken to eliminate the causes of a potential nonconformity, defect, or other undesirable situation in order to prevent occurrence.

**Problem Escalation**      The process of elevating a problem to appropriate management to aid in the resolution of the problem.

**Problem Report (PR)**      A problem report includes all forms of problem reporting from the customer such as written reports, letters, and telephone calls that are recorded manually or entered into an automated problem reporting tracking system.  A problem report or fault is assigned a severity level based on the nature of the problem or fault.  Problem reports include engineering reports.

**Problem Severity Level**      The classification of a problem based on its impact to predetermined criteria.

**Product**      Result of activities or processes.
  Notes:
1  A product may include service, hardware, processed materials, software or a combination thereof.
2  A product can be tangible (e.g. assemblies or processed materials) or intangible (e.g. knowledge  or concepts), or a combination thereof.
3  A product can be either intended (e.g.  offering to customers) or unintended (e.g. pollutant or unwanted effects).[6]

**Product Category/Class**      A specifically defined division of product which generally performs the same function(s).

**Program**      A planned, coordinated group of activities, procedure(s), etc., often for a specific purpose.

**Project**      A sequence of milestones and activities leading to a result over a prescribed set of time.

**Purchasing**      The process of obtaining a hardware, software, or services.

**Quality**      The totality of features and characteristics of a product  that bear on its ability to satisfy stated or implied needs.

**Quality Assurance**      All the planned and systematic activities implemented within the quality system and demonstrated as needed to provide adequate confidence that and entity will fulfill requirements for quality.

| | |
|---|---|
| **Quality Audit** | Systematic and independent examination to determine whether quality activities and related results comply with planned arrangements and whether these arrangements are implemented effectively and are suitable to achieve objectives. |
| **Quality Control** | Part of a quality management system focused on the operational techniques and processes used to fulfill quality requirements. |
| **Quality Improvement** | The actions taken to enhance the features and characteristics of products and to increase the effectiveness and efficiency of processes used to produce and deliver them. |
| **Quality Management** | All activities of the overall management function that determine the quality policy, objectives and responsibilities, and implement them by means such as quality planning, quality control, quality assurance and quality improvement within the quality system. |
| **Quality Management System** | Part of a management system related to the establishment and fulfillment of quality policy and quality objectives. |
| **Quality Plan** | A document setting out the specific quality practices, resources, and activities relevant to a particular product, process, service, contract, or project. |
| **Quality Planning** | Part of a quality management system focused on establishing and/or interpreting quality policy, quality objectives, and quality targets, quality requirements and defining how these are to be achieved. |
| **Quality Policy** | The overall quality intentions and direction of an organization with regard to quality as formally expressed by top management. |
| **Quality Surveillance** | The continuing monitoring and verification of the status of procedure(s), methods, conditions, products, processes, and services, and analysis of records in relation to stated references to ensure requirements for quality are being met. |
| **Quality System** | The organizational structure, responsibilities, procedure(s), processes, and resources for implementing quality management. |
| **QuEST Forum** | Quality Excellence for Suppliers of Telecommunications (QuEST Forum) is a partnership of telecommunications suppliers and service providers. The QuEST Forum's mission is developing and maintaining a common set of quality system requirements for the telecommunications industry worldwide, including reportable cost and performance-based metrics for the industry. |

**Reliability**
The ability of an item to perform a required function under stated conditions for a stated period of time.

**Repair**
The action taken on a nonconforming item so that it fulfills the intended usage requirements although it may not conform to the originally specified requirements.

**Replication**
The process of making copies from a master.

**Re-testing**
An activity in which a system or component is exercised under specified conditions, the results are observed or recorded, and an evaluation is made of the performance of the system or component.

**Risk Management**
A loss prevention methodology that encompasses identification and evaluation of risk, selection of risks to control, identification of preventive actions, cost benefit analysis and implementation of mitigating plans. Risk management is a pro-active approach for enabling business continuity.

**Service**
Result generated by activities at the interface between the supplier and the customer and by supplier internal activities to meet the customer needs.
NOTES:
1. The supplier or the customer may be represented at the interface by personnel or equipment;
2. Customer activities at the interface with the supplier may be essential to the service delivery;
3. Delivery or use of tangible products may form part of the service delivery; and
4. A service may be linked with the manufacture and supply of tangible product.[6]

**Service Provider**
See *Telecommunications Service Provider.*

**Software**
See *software product.*

**Software Product**
The set of computer programs, procedures, and possibly associated documentation and data.

NOTE: A software product may be designated for delivery, an integral part of another product, or used in the development process.

**Specification**
A document stating requirements.

**Subcontractor**
The organization that provides a product to the supplier. Same as *sub-supplier.*

**Subscriber**              Telecommunications Service Provider (TSP) Customer.

**Supplier**                A provider of Telecommunications Products.

**Support Software**        Software tools that are used in product development, manufacturing, and testing.

**System Test**             Testing conducted on a complete integrated system to evaluate the system's compliance with its specified requirements.

**Target Computer**         The computer on which delivered software is intended to operate.

**Telecommunications Service Provider**   Companies that supply telecommunications services to subscribers.

**Test Coverage**           The degree to which a test verifies a product's functions, sometimes expressed as a percent of functions tested.

**Test Plan**               Plan that describes the scope, strategy, and methodology for how to test.

**Testing**                 A means of determining an item's capability to meet specified requirements by subjecting them to a set of physical, chemical, environmental, or operating actions and conditions.

**TL 9000 Quality System Requirements Handbook**   A cooperative effort among members of the telecommunications industry in establishing a common set of quality system requirements built upon currently used industry standards, including the ISO 9000 series of international standards. The requirements promote consistency, efficiency, reduce redundancy and improve customer satisfaction.

**Traceability**            Ability to trace the history, application or location of an entity by means of recorded identifications.

**Validation**              Confirmation by examination and provision of objective evidence that the particular requirements for a specific intended use are fulfilled.

**Verification**            The act of reviewing, inspecting, testing, checking, auditing, or otherwise establishing and documenting whether items, processes, services, or documents conform to specified requirements.

**Virus, Software**     A computer program, usually hidden within another seemingly innocuous program, which produces copies of itself and inserts them into other programs and that usually performs a malicious action (such as destroying data).

**Work Instructions**     Sometimes referred to as local procedure(s), work instructions provide details of "how" work is performed.

# Bibliography and Endnote Reference

[1]  ISO Q10011-1-94  *Guidelines for Auditing Quality Systems - Auditing*, Milwaukee, American Society for Quality Control, 1994.

[2]  ISO Q10011-2-94  *Guidelines for Auditing Quality Systems - Qualification Criteria for Quality Systems Auditors*, Milwaukee, American Society for Quality Control, 1994.

[3]  ISO Q10011-3-94  *Guidelines for Auditing Quality Systems - Management of Audit Programs*, Milwaukee, American Society for Quality Control, 1994.

[4]  GR-1202-CORE  *Generic Requirements for a Customer Sensitive Quality Infrastructure*, Morristown, New Jersey, Telcordia Technologies, Issue 1, October 1995.

[5]  GR-1252-CORE  *Quality System Generic Requirements for Hardware*, Morristown, New Jersey, Telcordia Technologies, Issue 1, May 1995.

[6]  ISO 8402:1994  *Quality Management and Assurance – Vocabulary*, Geneva, Switzerland, International Organization for Standardization

[7]  ISO 9001:1994  *Quality Systems - Model for Quality Assurance in Design/ Development, Production, Installation and Servicing*, Geneva, Switzerland, International Organization for Standardization, Second Edition, 1994.

[8]  ISO 9000-3:1997  *Quality Management and Quality Assurance Standards - Part 3: Guidelines for the Application of ISO 9001:1994 to the Development Supply, Installation, and Maintenance of Computer Software, 1997,* Geneva, Switzerland, International Organization for Standardization, Second Edition, 1994

[9]  ISO / IEC 12207  *Information Technology Software Life Cycle Processes,* Geneva Switzerland, International Organization for Standardization, February 1995.

**[10]**    TR-NWT-000179              *Quality System Generic Requirements for Software*, Morristown, New Jersey, Telcordia Technologies, Issue 2, June 1993.

**[11]**    QS-9000                        *Quality System Requirements QS-9000,* Detroit, Michigan, Automotive Industry Action Group (AIAG), 3rd Edition, March 1998.

**[12]**    ISO 9004-2:1994          *Quality management and quality system elements – Part 2: Guidelines for Services,* Geneva, Switzerland, International Organization for Standardization, 1994